Hooligar

by

Joanna Currey and David M. Kennedy

Based on the book *Try for the Gold* by Mark Ryan

American Rugby Story, LLC

Charlottesville, VA

Published in the United State by American Rugby Story, LLC
www.americanrugbystory.com
HG11 scriptment 2018-R64
Second eBook edition: October 2018

Cover photo: Captains and referee, USA versus France, 1924, Paris, courtesy of Frederick Humbert

10, 9, 8, 7, 6, 5, 4, 3, 2, 1
ISBN 978-1-7294586-0-0
eBook ISBN 978-1-7329032-0-3

Contents

Copyright 1
Preface 3
Acknowledgements 6
Introduction 7
Logline & Characters 8
Scriptment 10
Keep Going 176

Preface

About ARS and scrum storytelling

American Rugby Story, LLC is a film development company. We work exclusively on feature films based upon true stories.

ARS's special sauce is scrum storytelling, a film development method that pumps more believability value into screenplays. Scrum storytelling taps the clarity of the crowd, representing various demographics across numerous iterations.

Our role in the filmmaking process is distinct from that of film production companies. ARS is involved in the beginning stages of a film: we identify compelling and inspirational true stories and acquire film rights to related book(s). Next, we raise six figure development financing while performing extensive supplemental research. Afterwards, ARS generates scene-by-scene outlines and treatments, then hires Hollywood screenwriters to evolve them into scripts. Along the way we expose ARS screenplay work products to reviewer scrums (demographically diverse groups of reviewers from both film and non-film backgrounds) to gather layers of crucial feedback as we go.

ARS occasionally also develops scriptments—hybrid scripts and treatments. Treatments typically run 30 pages, and full scripts 120 pages. Acting like midway stepping-stones, our scriptments range from 60 to 90 pages.

Scrum storytelling is a three-year development process. During select writing stages, ARS producers and interns assist writers extensively, performing the preparatory and post-writing steps. This allows writers to focus more on their artistry and less on peripheral tasks. As the stories in our care mature, ARS markets and sells its intellectual property bundles (e.g. film rights to the book, research documents, outlines, scene-by-scene specification documents, treatment, scriptment and script) to a production entity.

Clarification

Scrum storytelling reliably breaks huge screenwriting projects into more atomic pieces that allow for workload sharing and more focused artistry. It also shares the burden of revision among many minds, compiling collective reactions to each evolution of a project into streamlined feedback. Scrum storytelling helps maintain audience immersion by way of credibility triangulation. In other words, we take special care to avoid storytelling screeches, skips and other shortcomings.

All that stated, scrum storytelling does not replace talented Hollywood screenwriters. Rather, it provides powerful information that allows development teams, including professional writers, to see better, more believable ways to tell stories.

ARS provides scrum storytelling insights as suggestions to A-list screenwriters. We understand that these are merely supplements to the traditional and essential storytelling magic that will always be the domain of writers.

Why ARS publishes scriptments via Amazon

1. Andy Weir (*The Martian*, *Artemis*) encouraged us to follow in his footsteps

2. It provides easier access to A-list Hollywood screenwriters who are candidate vendors
3. It provides easier access to producers who are candidate screenplay acquiring customers
4. Scriptments are easier for non-professionals to read than scripts because they're more like books
5. It provides easier access to consumers who may become grass-roots *green light* promoters

How friends of HG can help it get made

a. Buy the scriptment for the $1.00 Amazon minimum to help with the Hooligans Game stats
b. Read the 90-ish pages and rate HG on Amazon
c. Tell your friends

Contact

Agents for candidate A-list screenwriters or candidate screenplay acquiring producers should contact:
Bob Pflug
Development Producer
bob@americanrugbystory.com
315-406-9927

Acknowledgements

We at ARS appreciate the Hooligans Game clarifying feedback contributed by so many reviewers: women and men, young and old, content aware and unaware.

Introduction

Hooligans Game is not a film about rugby. It's a film about PTSD set against a backdrop of the 1924 Olympics rugby competition.

Since the onset of the 21st century, veteran suicides have increased 31 percent, and suicides among U.S. civilian adults have increased 24 percent (U.S. Department of Veteran Affairs, 2016). Post-Traumatic Stress Disorder (PTSD) has often been associated with the 21st century U.S. suicide epidemic and other sufferings of veterans, survivors of sexual assault and victims of other extreme trauma.

Logline and Characters

Logline

In 1924, a withdrawn WWI veteran named Colby Slater joins a group of collegiate basketball, baseball, and football players who have come together to compete in the Olympic rugby competition. Once in Paris, the boys must reckon with the dominant French team and violent French fans, while Colby reckons with his traumatic past. (Based on a true story.)

Characters

Colby Slater - A tall quiet farmer, WWI veteran, and reluctant rugby captain
Rudy Scholz - A short, vocal lawyer, rugby veteran and team organizer
James Peters - The black English assistant coach of the backs
Ed Turk Turkington - A former track star and handsome rugby rookie with wandering eyes
Charles Austin - The gruff head coach
Louise Slater – A wise, resilient homemaker, widow and mother of Colby and Norman
Lucia Garrison Norton - A confident, adventuresome recent graduate of Smith College with unflinching progressive political views
John O'Neil - A rich oilman and gritty and courageous rugby veteran with a slight build
Pierre de Coubertin - An idealistic baron and rugby enthusiast who founded the modern Olympics
Charlie Roe - The unscrupulous rugby veteran obsessed with becoming vice-captain

Norman Slater - Colby's intrepid older brother and rugby veteran
Caesar Mannelli - A stocky, happy baseball center fielder and rugby rookie born in Italy

Scriptment

"Rugby is a hooligans game played by gentlemen."

-Sir Winston Churchill (apocryphal)

"What is admirable in rugby is the perpetual mix of individualism and discipline, the necessity for each to think, anticipate, take a decision and at the same time subordinate one's reasoning, thoughts and decisions."

-Pierre de Coubertin, founder of the modern Olympic Games

FADE IN:

INT. STAIRCASE - NIGHT

SERIES OF SHOTS:

-A TEENAGE BOY hesitantly climbs a creaky staircase

TEENAGE BOY'S VOICE (V.O.)
"The weakest step
toward the top of the hill,
toward sunrise, toward
hope"

-Teenage Boy reaches for the bedroom doorknob

TEENAGE BOY'S VOICE (V.O.)
"is stronger than the
fiercest storm."

-CRACK! Catatonic Teenage Boy shivers by the railing

TEENAGE BOY'S VOICE (V.O.)
"Keep going."

EXT. SLATERS SHATTUCK AVE HOME - DAY

TITLE OVER: December 1907

TITLE OVER: Based on a true story

In the early morning light, eleven-year-old COLBY SLATER smiles, breeze blowing his blonde hair. He's standing on the widow's walk of a grand mid-town Berkley home.

Because fog mostly obscures his view, Colby crouches to peer out over the bay. Suddenly, his face lights up and he turns and runs into the house.

INT. SECOND FLOOR HALLWAY - DAY [CONTINUOUS]

Colby turns his head as he runs past NORMAN SLATER reading a newspaper in their shared bedroom.

COLBY (SHOUTING)
Dad's home!

Two years older and confident in his greater wisdom, Norman disagrees.

NORMAN
Tell it to Sweeney! It's too early.

BOYS' ROOM

Sixteen-year-old MARGUERITE SLATER appears in Norman's doorway, asking about the commotion.

MARGUERITE
Everything alright?

NORMAN (STARING DOWN AT PAPER)
Californians went and did what President Roosevelt only threatened. They banned football!

MARGUERITE
Good riddance. But I meant is everything alright with *your* brother.

NORMAN (SHRUGGING)
YOUR brother sees Dad on every ship crossing the bay.

FATHER'S STUDY

Crashing downstairs and into his father's study, Colby pauses in front of a large desk. On it there are neatly arranged books, papers, a globe, a lamp, and an old brass spyglass on a stand. Colby hesitates, then grabs the spyglass.

SECOND FLOOR HALLWAY

Colby dashes back towards the widow's walk, urging Norman to follow. Norman rolls his eyes and gets up from the bed.

EXT. WIDOW'S WALK - DAY [CONTINUOUS]

Colby looks through the spyglass towards the bay. Norman snatches it away and searches the bay himself. His face morphs into surprise.

NORMAN
You're right Colby, that's *Charmer*!

Norman pans right from *Charmer* at bow to half-mast flag at stern.

EXT. SLATERS SHATTUCK AVE HOME - DAY

People formally dressed make their way around a fancy horse-drawn hearse to enter the Slater home.

INT. UPSTAIRS BEDROOM - DAY [CONTINUOUS]

It's late afternoon. Resilient forty-year-old, LOUISE SLATER, perseveres as she helps her younger children. She fixes the part in Norman's rigid hair and straightens

Colby's collar. All are silent and expressionless in their shared grief.

INT. LIVING ROOM - DAY

The Captain John Slater funeral attendees sing a hymn. The Slater family stands in front. Tears roll down Louise's face as she and Norman sing. Marguerite nudges Norman, nodding towards Colby.

Colby seems unaware of his surroundings. He isn't singing, and his expression remains vacant.

EXT. SLATERS SHATTUCK AVE HOME - DAY

Louise searches for Colby as the procession readies to leave for the burial site in Oakland. Colby sits curled up on the widow's walk, staring at its spindles. The sun hangs low over the bay, its light glinting off the lens of the spyglass discarded by Colby's side.

LOUISE (LOOKING AROUND)
Where are you? Colby?
Colby!

EXT. SLATERS HASTE ST HOME - DAY

TITLE OVER: September 1911

During the four years since Captain John Slater died, Louise was forced to sell the family home. Now the Slaters live in a humble, cramped house on Haste Street.

Louise opens the front door and shoos Colby out.

LOUISE
Go fish in the bay or watch your brother's scrimmage. Just get some fresh air and stop sulking around.

DURANT AVENUE

Slowly and sullenly, Colby wanders down Durant Ave.

RUGBY FIELD

Eventually, he arrives at the chain-link fence surrounding the varsity field. He looks perturbed, as if he arrived there by accident. Colby leans his forehead against the fence, looking down. He kicks the grass while fiddling with a broken link. Action sounds come from the field, and then crescendo. Head still down, he listens intently. The sounds erupt into a loud, violent collision and Colby looks up. (See Apx B shot.)

EXT. BERKELEY HIGH - DAY

TITLE OVER: Two months later

Colby is playing wing, running along the sideline in support of Norman who has the ball. Norman takes a hit but barrels through.

About to run into more trouble, Norman passes to Colby, switching behind him. Colby dodges one defender, and with two more converging he makes a long, difficult pass to a BERKELEY HIGH TEAMMATE just before impact.

The crowd, dressed in sweaters and light jackets, is cheering, getting louder. An INCREDULOUS MAN in the bleachers looks impressed and asks who Colby is. Louise, standing in the row behind him, overhears and cracks a proud smile.

Berkeley High Teammate scores a try, but it's called back as a forward pass. Clapping and cheering, then booing and stomping erupt in waves from the crowd.

CROWD NOISE FROM GAME FADES INTO RUMBLING AND BUMPING OF AN ARMY AMBULANCE ON A PLANK ROAD

EXT. FORMER BATTLEFIELD - DAY

TITLE OVER: 1918 - Passchendaele, Belgium

Spotting a washed-away section of planks, Colby, now an Army medic, brings his Ford army ambulance to a stop on the plank road (see Apx. C pic). His face is sullen. In the passenger seat slumps a wounded U.S. soldier, a DOUGHBOY who has been shot in the hand. Turning off the road and onto a less traveled dirt path, Colby drives onward.

A ways down the trail, Doughboy perks up and squints at something through the windshield. He points. Colby looks and sees a crumpled shape in a filthy but just distinguishable British army uniform lying near the rim of some kind of pit. Wordlessly, he pulls the ambulance over to a squeaky stop. Colby grabs his medic pack from the running board and steps out to see if it's another wounded soldier in need of help. Doughboy follows.

COLBY

Grab your gun.

Doughboy backpedals, pokes his head through the Ford's storm curtain and grabs his M1903 Springfield rifle. They walk to the face-down body and turn it over, discovering it's a mostly decomposed skeleton in uniform. Colby's face contorts.

They take a few more steps towards the pit and lean over to look inside. It's a vast bomb crater littered with long-dead German and English soldiers, some still clutching rusty weapons.

Colby is distressed. Doughboy thrusts his gun into Colby's arms and begins climbing backwards down into the crater, holding a tree root with his good hand.

DOUGHBOY

I'm gettin' myself a souvenir.

With a dry snap, the root Doughboy is holding breaks and he slides down the slope, bumping and disturbing several bodies as he comes to a halt.

Doughboy bends over to remove a dead German's spiked helmet. Colby stares at a partially skeletonized soldier still holding his rifle. Doughboy screams. A few yards away, the alpha rat screams in return as he and many others scurry towards Doughboy.

DOUGHBOY (YELLING)
Pull me out! Pull me out!

Colby drops the rifle and reaches down into the crater to pull Doughboy out. Doughboy spasmodically kicks a few rats from his legs. Up top, Doughboy releases Colby and scoops up his rifle. They sprint towards the ambulance.

A safe distance away, they slow to a walk. His panic fading, Doughboy begins to chuckle between panting breaths. He hands Colby the helmet, seemingly oblivious to how disturbed Colby looks, and cracks a joke about his souvenir.

Back at the ambulance, Colby turns and gazes sullenly at the spiked helmet in his hand, then beyond it towards the crater.

CRACK! Colby jumps visibly, whipping his head around to see Doughboy standing slightly behind him, smoking rifle resting across the forearm of his wounded hand. Doughboy has shot a rat that made it out of the crater. He guffaws triumphantly.

DOUGHBOY
Take that, Wilhelm! Haha. Did ya see how high he flew?

INT. PIERRE'S OFFICE - DAY

THIS SCENE IS SPOKEN IN FRENCH WITH ENGLISH SUBTITLES.

TITLE OVER: November 1923 - Paris, France

PIERRE DE COUBERTIN, a man in his sixties with a bushy white mustache, is the founder of the modern Olympics. Pierre is an idealist who has spent most of his personal fortune developing the Games. He paces in his office distractedly, hands clasped behind his back. He stops to look out his office window towards the Arc de Triomphe.

PIERRE
...but the Games cannot happen without rugby! And we cannot have a rugby event with only France and Romania competing. Who else did you invite?

Former French Rugby star, Forty-one-year-old ALLAN MUHR, is sitting matter-of-factly with his arms crossed. He sighs, watching his friend pace in an all too familiar scenario. Muhr explains again why he and his French Olympic Committee were unable to attract the British.

MUHR
They say, "no." Our Five Nations tournament partners say French players are ungentlemanly and we play dirty. (beat) And, as you know, the southern hemisphere teams are having trouble getting here by May.

Muhr further observes that the American Olympic Association (AOA) has no motivation to dedicate the resources necessary to field a team. Too few American rugby players remain after American football was reformed, and the competition could only result in national embarrassment.

Pierre insists something must be done.

PIERRE
The Olympic spirit and the rugby spirit are about participation, struggling, collaboration, honor and sportsmanship. This American committee seems to believe it's about politics and

manipulating outcomes!
France and the world
need a rugby approach!

Muhr sighs. He's heard this speech countless times.

MUHR
The Americans will not
come. They have no
rugby, no team to send.

Pierre looks resolute, reaching for his stationary.

PIERRE
Then they will have to
create one. And I will tell
them so.

INT. SAN FRANCISCO CABLE CAR - DAY

TITLE OVER: Two weeks later - San Francisco, California

CHARLES AUSTIN, a middle-aged former rugby coach, rides in a crowded cable car. His demeanor is grumpy and stand-offish. While other passengers chat loudly, Austin distractedly chomps a fat cigar. There's shouting as someone tries to ride without a token.

EXT. STREETS OF SAN FRANCISCO - DAY
[CONTINUOUS]

He exits onto the street quickly and makes his way through downtown San Francisco. He has to duck, dodge, spin, and scramble around people, cars, movers, opening and closing shop doors, revisiting some of his old rugby prowess and getting more and more irritated as his journey continues. Finally, Austin arrives at a large building containing the law offices of Rudy Scholz.

As he's about to step into the revolving door, a DISCOURTEOUS MAN bumps past him, knocking the cigar out of his hand. Austin aggressively stomps his cigar out, now thoroughly furious just in time to meet with Rudy.

INT. SCHOLZ LAW OFFICES - DAY

RUDY SCHOLZ, a fiery, audacious 5'6" lawyer, explains to Austin his backup plan. Now that AOA has refused to sponsor a rugby team, Rudy proposes that he and Austin raise money and hold rugby tryouts themselves.

They've been talking at length and the power of Austin's skepticism is meeting its match in Rudy's silver tongue.

AUSTIN

It's what, a decade since football got unbanned? Even if we could find guys with rugby experience, they'd be pushin' thirty. It's suicide.

The lawyer rebuts, pointing-out that he's pushing thirty himself, yet still in good shape. And he insists that the fundraising will be no problem. Rudy believes everyone will fall in love with the underdogs, the unlikely American heroes. Austin reluctantly agrees on the condition that they drop the idea if not enough candidates tryout. Rudy is happy he's won Austin over, and promises to write an ad for the paper right away, as well as a response letter to the International Olympic Committee (IOC).

EXT. SAN FRANCISCO NEWS KIOSK - DAY

Track star, ED *TURK* TURKINGTON, and a BUDDY are browsing at a newsstand. Turk spots an ad for the tryouts.

TURK
Hot dawg! They need guys to come out for the Olympic rugby team!

Buddy peeks over Turk's shoulder at the ad.

BUDDY
I don't know. Just 'cause you can make a sap of anyone running the 220 doesn't mean you can up and win at every sport you try. And even if you get picked, what about Elaine?

TURK (STARING AT THE PAPER)
We're engaged. She's
stuck on me; it'll be fine.

THE ADVERTISEMENT DETAILS FLASH ACROSS THE SCREEN

INT. NEW YORK - AMERICAN OLYMPIC ASSOCIATION OFFICE - DAY

Four members of the AOA, all mature men, are debating whether or not to allow Rudy and Austin's theoretical team to compete in Paris. Some argue that it's all a setup, that France is pushing so hard for them to compete because they want to embarrass the U.S.

Huffy AOA MEMBER 1 slaps a copy of the New York Times on the conference table in front of CHARLES DYER NORTON.

AOA MEMBER 1
Who tries to send an
Olympic team for a sport
we don't play? And why
are these guys
circumventing us?

AOA MEMBER 4 squeezes behind AOA MEMBER 2's chair to look over AOA Member 1's shoulder.

AOA MEMBER 4

This came through the AP wire from The Chronicle. Is the whole rugby team from San Francisco?

AOA MEMBER 1

There is no team!

Mr. Norton picks up the paper and holds it to his face.

MR. NORTON

Not entirely. But a few Bay Area colleges are cited as former rugby hotbeds.

Mr. Norton tosses the paper into his open briefcase.

MR. NORTON

Speaking of colleges, I need to leave early. Katherine and I are driving up to Smith to collect Lucia.

AOA MEMBER 2

We must come to a conclusion.

MR. NORTON

Certainly, we can field a team. Didn't we win a medal in Antwerp?

AOA MEMBER 1
That was a fluke. It was muddy, and our guys were too big to push in the muck. And rugby had only been extinct four or five years, so more U.S. boys were young enough to play and old enough to remember how!

MR. NORTON
But we won.

AOA Member 1 shakes his head with a condescending grimace.

AOA MEMBER 1
We only won because of a ringer Australian, Danny Clark. And, like... I... said... THE MUD. A week later, after it stopped raining, France stomped us in a rematch.

AOA MEMBER 2
This is 1923. It's absurd to form a team now.

Why do these
Californians want to?

An ASSISTANT with bobbed hair quietly knocks before entering the room to whisper in Mr. Norton's ear. Mr. Norton gathers his briefcase and coat.

MR. NORTON
Who knows? Maybe
they'll find some younger
athletes who can pick up
rugby with ease. Why
not try?

AOA MEMBER 1
That's preposterous!
Have you ever seen a
rugby game? You can't
just send basketball and
football players, even
great ones, and expect
them to win. They will
make fools of
themselves.

AOA MEMBER 4 (NODDING)
Maybe. Or they might
stick it to the French,
American-style.

AOA MEMBER 2

If the AOA disassociates
ourselves with the team,
who really cares?

The members reluctantly agree to let the team try, figuring it's highly unlikely Rudy and Austin raise enough funds.

EXT. SMITH COLLEGE - DAY

Academically advanced LUCIA GARRISON NORTON has finished her bachelor's degree in three and a half years. She's bundled up and it's snowing lightly.

Her parents pull up in a Packard, waving lovingly. Mr. Norton hops out of the still running car, kisses Lucia on the cheek, and begins to wrestle her Louis Vuitton steamer trunk into the back seat. (See Apx. C pics.)

KAT NORTON mentions how beautiful and well Lucia looks.

MRS. NORTON
Now, darling, are you
sure you won't
reconsider walking with
your class in May? Don't
you want to be with your
friends? We were so
looking forward to your
graduation.

Mr. Norton is getting red in the face from flipping the large trunk this way and that to make it fit with enough room for Lucia to sit beside it. Lucia helps from the other side.

MRS. NORTON

You could visit Paris the next spring instead.

LUCIA

No, mother. We've discussed this. The Olympics are happening *this* year and I'd rather not wait until 1928.

Lucia glances at the newspaper that Mr. Norton spread across the back seat to protect it from the luggage. Seeing the article about the U.S. rugby team, she opportunistically feigns interest in an attempt to quiet her mother.

LUCIA (EMPHATICALLY)

I'm anxious to see our rugby team compete! You and Daddy are *so* kind to give me this trip. Ceremonies are for people with stiff collars. Graduated is graduated.

Mrs. Norton sighs, knowing there's no convincing her bright, loving, yet stubborn daughter.

MRS. NORTON
Well at least we know you'll be safe in France. Luella wrote and said she's just ecstatic to host you and show you *her* Paris.

Lucia smiles and the Packard pulls away.

EXT. EWING FIELD - DAY

TITLE OVER: December 23, 1923 - First day of try outs

SERIES OF SHOTS (various sports):

-CAESAR MANNELLI, a jovial, stocky Italian-American stands at bat

-WILLIAM "LEFTY" ROGERS, the confident, agile captain of the Stanford basketball team, sinks a jump shot

-LINN FARISH, a socially awkward yet athletic and intelligent linebacker, launches into an intimidating gallop

Nineteen-year-old ELAINE HORTON has come to cheer on her fiancé Turk among 200 other spectators at the tryouts. Roughly 85 prospective players have arrived.

Austin is attempting to run a scrimmage. Nothing is going right. He sees many clumsy missed tackles, bad passes, and knock-ons. An assistant coach from New Zealand, BIG JIM WYLIE, shakes his head. Players are getting frustrated and Austin, barking orders, is exasperated.

Austin, Rudy and Wylie decide to start again at the very beginning. They gather the rugby rookies and veterans alike and Austin starts giving a rundown of the essential rules of rugby while Rudy and Wylie look on.

Rookie Linn Farish wears padded football pants and a tattered shirt.

FARISH

Forward passing is illegal?

AUSTIN

Right. Only sideways or backwards.

Austin zips an underhand pass with the ball he's been holding to Rudy, standing a few yards to his left.

FARISH

Are we allowed to make overhand passes to the side?

RUDY (GRINNING)

Be my guest. But just so you know, there's no blocking in rugby. After

you get plastered a few
times you'll figure out
the underhand is a lot
quicker. Also, rugby
players don't wear pads!

Austin moves on to the player positions. Turk, trying not to crack a smile, whispers to Caesar.

TURK

How'd you like to be the
hooker?

Tall, Irish-American veteran, JACK PATRICK, rolls his eyes.

PATRICK

Good one, rookie, no
one's ever made that joke
before.

Austin wraps up and they begin low level drills, line drills, passing, and tackling. Everything is much more basic, but the rookies are catching on.

Rudy pulls Patrick aside.

RUDY

Any idea where Colby
Slater is?

Patrick shrugs.

RUDY
Damn, we could really use him.

CUT TO:

INT. WOODLAND, CA - SLATER FARM - SAME

Colby hears a knock. He stands slowly like a much older man, walks in wool socks to his foyer, and cautiously opens the door. Louise greets and hugs him. She's come for Christmas.

They walk into the dining room to find Norman eating chicken. He snuck in through the kitchen door when Colby went to the front. The tiniest hint of a smirk crosses Colby's face.

COLBY (QUIET)
I don't remember inviting you to come eat all my food.

NORMAN
You didn't. If I stopped inviting myself I'd forget how you look and starve to death!

LOUISE
Shhh. Come help me make lunch. Colby, fetch

some eggs. Norman,
clean up all these dishes.

Later, during lunch, Louise recognizes a quiet moment.

LOUISE
I saw an article about
some Olympic tryouts
happening in the city.
(beat) Rugby tryouts.

Colby doesn't respond.

NORMAN
I heard about that too.
Old Rudy Scholz is
involved in it.

Louise continues to look at Colby.

LOUISE
I bet they'd love it if you
showed up.

Colby mumbles something dismissive. While Norman has eaten his lunch and is going for more, Colby's plate is virtually untouched. Colby grabs the water jug and exits again.

BACK TO:

EXT. EWING FIELD - SAME

There's some horseplay on the field as rookies get more comfortable. Players deliver surprise tackles to each other's backs and wrestle on the ground. In one drill, Turk handles a pass clumsily before showing off his amazing speed by outpacing several defenders to score.

Another rookie, RICHARD "TRICKY DICK" HYLAND, shows off his own impressive speed and agility. The Stanford halfback aspires to out-perform Turk.

LEFTY
You're a regular Jim Thorpe, Dick.

HYLAND
Jim Thorpe ain't got my swerve.

Though interest is high, by the end of tryouts, Austin, Rudy and Wylie have their doubts about whether they can shape raw athleticism into a true rugby team in time.

EXT. PARK OVERLOOKING THE BAY - DAY

Turk and Elaine sit on a bench facing the bay. The sun hangs low in the sky, glimmering off the water and casting soft golden light. The bench is decorated with a big red bow and a lamp post nearby has a wreath attached. Turk takes Elaine's hands in his.

TURK

Elaine, you know this is hard for me. It's not that I don't love you, but I just can't be distracted if I'm going to train my best for Paris.

Elaine is shocked and speechless. She looks away, a few silent tears rolling down her cheeks as she tries to keep her composure. She pulls her hands out of his and wipes her eyes. Eventually, she clears her throat and looks at Turk.

ELAINE

You're sure?

TURK

Well, maybe I won't need as long a break if I don't get selected.

Elaine looks away again, taking a deep breath. Turk proposes they meet back at the same bench in exactly six months if both want to try again.

ELAINE (SOFTLY)

I love you and I want this to work. But I won't be your contingency plan.

Elaine takes off her engagement ring and hands it to Turk.

EXT. SLATER FARM - DAY

Louise walks across Colby's property carrying the day's mail. She steps through a side door into the kitchen.

INT. KITCHEN - DAY [CONTINUOUS]

Now thirty-two and married, Marguerite Slater Messenger is sitting at the small kitchen table sipping tea. Mother and daughter chat.

Louise places Colby's mail on the counter and starts opening cabinets, looking for sugar for her own tea. She comes across an entire shelf full of unopened mail. Shocked, Louise pulls it out and remarks on how old some of it is. She and Marguerite talk about how worried they are about Colby and how increasingly distant he seems.

Louise hones in on the name *Rudy Scholz* scrawled across the return address of one envelope and begins to open it. Marguerite asks if she really should be doing that, and Louise counters that the letter was sent to be opened, and if she didn't, nobody would.

MARGUERITE
Where is he anyway? I
haven't seen him for a
few hours now.

Louise, pouring over the letter, doesn't look up.

MARGUERITE

Who's it from, mama?

Louise folds up the letter.

LOUISE
One of your brother's old
rugby mates. I'm going
to go find him.

EXT. SLATER FARM - DAY [CONTINUOUS]

Louise leaves the kitchen and walks towards a large equipment shed. The bay door is open but she can't see inside the shady shed with her eyes still adjusting to the bright outdoors.

INT. EQUIPMENT SHED - DAY [CONTINUOUS]

Louise slowly enters. A rooster just behind the door clucks and flaps its wings. Startled, Louise jumps back and catches the sleeve of her city dress on a nail.

LOUISE (FLUSTERED)
Colby! Are you in here?

Hearing a wrench clink, she continues onward and stumbles over a grain seeder (see Apx. C pic) in her city shoes. Colby's strong hand catches her arm. Surprised, she stares at him for a moment, then he crouches back down to continue tinkering with a piece of farm equipment.

Regaining her composure, Louise pulls the letter out of her apron pocket, asking if he ever intended to open it and if he knew why Rudy wrote. Colby shrugs.

COLBY
Doesn't matter.

Louise tells him that Rudy has written specifically to Colby saying they want him for the Olympic rugby team. Becoming tender, she says that it *does* matter. Their family has been through enough and she's worried about Colby.

COLBY
I'm too old for rugby.

LOUISE
Bah. Norman's 30, and he's game.

Colby glances at her then looks back at his work.

COLBY
Need to tend to the farm.

LOUISE
You have a sister who graduated from University Farm School, just like you. With honors! I think she and I can feed the sheep.

Colby glances up once more, then shifts his eyes to Louise's torn sleeve. Louise sighs, exasperated.

INT. PIERRE'S OFFICE - DAY

THIS SCENE IS SPOKEN IN FRENCH WITH ENGLISH SUBTITLES.

Pierre has learned that the AOA won't help organize or sponsor a rugby team and is discouraged. Muhr tries to lighten the mood.

MUHR

Ah, but you know of the rebellious American spirit.

Pierre will not be placated. He wants a united front from all nations participating in the games, giving the Olympics and rugby the reverence they deserve. Looking out again towards the Arc, Pierre's mind wanders.

BEGIN FLASHBACK:

EXT. THE RUGBY SCHOOL - DAY

TITLE OVER: 1886 - Warwickshire, England

Pierre is visiting an English prep school to conduct academic research. Leaving its library, he happens across a rugby game outside. Pierre is mesmerized by the violent yet cooperative game. He excitedly scribbles his observations on a notepad.

PIERRE’S VOICE (V.O.)
Rugby is concerned with the mix of individualism and discipline. Each autonomous player functioning as part of a greater whole.

Pierre watches as one player lies over the injured knee of his opponent, protecting him until the ruck concludes.

PIERRE'S VOICE (V.O.)
No single player can succeed alone but must trust in others, showing respect for the greater good of the team, of the game, of all.

END FLASHBACK.

PIERRE
These Americans must come.

Pierre resolves to send a telegram to Rudy and Austin, encouraging them and insisting U.S. participation is of the utmost importance to the IOC and the host nation of France. He also resolves to send one to the AOA for good measure.

MUHR (UNDER HIS BREATH)

My goodness; not again.

INT. SCHOLZ LAW OFFICES - DAY

Rudy's holding the telegram from Pierre.

RUDY
"We will be eternally grateful to you for sending a United States team to the Olympic Rugby Competition... the entire Olympic and French communities await your response, which if negative, will result in deep disappointment."

Rudy shakes his head.

RUDY
So the chances of us making this happen are low. No one believes we can organize a team, raise the cabbage, train the players and make it to the pitch in Paris.

AUSTIN
Low? We're lousy with rookie kids. We'd need to

turn Keystone Cops into
Rough Riders in a matter
of months.

RUDY

Sure, sure. But look
around you for heaven's
sake. Everything in this
world is for sale.

Austin's brow begins to rise.

RUDY

But not these games. The
Olympics. Amateurs
only. Fair competition.
Not for hire. Not for sale.

AUSTIN (NODDING TENTATIVELY)

Like the gentlemen who
play rugby.

RUDY (ROTATING IN CHAIR)

Exactly! And that
gentlemen stuff, it
threatens some people:
political people, the
money-mongers and the
power-grabbers.

AUSTIN (EYES LOWERED)

But keeps other people
goin'.

Rudy turns back to Austin, decisive.

RUDY
It keeps you, me, and
maybe old Coubertin
going, anyway. I say...

Austin looks up at Rudy's face.

RUDY
...we set aside all the
reasons not to and just do
this.

Austin looks pensive, then laughs and leans forward warily. Rudy laughs too. The men shake.

AUSTIN
What the hell.

INT. SLATER FARM - DINING ROOM - DAY

Louise reads a newspaper out loud. Norman is munching peanuts from a bowl on the coffee table and listening.

An article from Harry Hayward says that Rudy Scholz and company are holding a second round of tryouts.

LOUISE
"Although rugby has
been supposedly dead
for...years, the love for

the game has been
smoldering in the hearts
of everybody who ever
played."

Inspired again, Louise calls Colby into the room and urges him to attend these tryouts, appealing to his sense of patriotic duty.

Colby's eyes are tired and downcast. He leans against the wall, squares of sunlight from a window illuminating half his body and face.

COLBY
I've already been over
there... for my country.

Louise's tone turns more empathetic and exhausted.

LOUISE
I know, dear. And I lost
husbands, you lost
fathers.

Colby snaps his head up and locks eyes with Louise.

LOUISE
Between our family's
tragedies and the war,
you've seen more death
than anyone should. And
you were too young.
(beat) But I know how

your face looks when
you play rugby. It looks
like you've found peace.

Norman crunches a few more times and swallows.

NORMAN
I'll go if you go.

LOUISE (QUIETLY)
It's the first day of the
new year, Colby. Things
will change if we have
faith. I want to see that
look on your face again.

Colby thinks for a long time. He absentmindedly walks over to the coffee table and grabs and eats a few peanuts.

EXT. EWING FIELD - DAY

There are 30 or 40 prospective players left, hard at work running drills. After declaring a water break Austin looks up from his clipboard and squints at the parking lot.

Colby and Norman are walking onto the practice field in the bright California sun. Rudy looks up too, spotting his old friend. He yells out towards the Slaters.

RUDY
Whaddya know.
Colossus finally shows.

Oilman JOHN O'NEIL, a wealthy 25-year-old, jogs from the parking lot to catch up with the Slaters. He stands on tiptoe to wrap his arms around their shoulders.

The Slaters and O'Neil reach Austin and they shake hands all around. Austin looks pleased. Colby looks down the field past Austin, making eye contact with Rudy and nods. Rudy smiles and nods, walking toward the group.

RUDY
John, the fundraising
committee appreciates--

O'NEIL
Rudy, old boy! Sorry to
miss the first tryout; I
was drilling in Montana.

O'Neil jogs over to Rudy, offers his hand and leans in.

O'NEIL (HUSHED)
It's my pleasure to
contribute, Rudy. But I'd
appreciate you keeping
that between us.

O'Neil winks. Rudy nods in accordance, then turns to the Slaters and points at his wrist.

RUDY
Not sure how they tell
time on the farm, maybe

sundials. But you're late! Everybody back on the field!

Austin instructs the backs to come with him and Rudy, and the pack to go with Coach Wylie. O'Neil overhears a brand-new rookie expressing confusion. Chicago native, DUDLEY *DUD* DEGROOT, is the largest person on the field. O'Neil introduces himself and pegs Dud as a lock, part of the pack. (See Apx. B shot.)

O'NEIL

It's not that different from football linemen for the forwards (i.e. pack). I play hooker which is like the ball-snapping center. Big squatty guys like Mannelli line up as props on either side of me during scrums. So they're like guards in football. Make sense?

DUD

Yeah. Okay.

O'NEIL

And big tall guys like you are locks. Locks are like tackles except in rugby scrums the *tackles* line-up behind the *guards* and me, for good pushing. Bound onto the locks are flankers, like ends in football. But because rugby players are both offensive and defensive, I'd say they're more like linebackers.

DUD

Like that tall guy you walked up with?

O'NEIL

Sort of. More like his brother. Colby plays 8 and there's no good football analogy for eight-man. But, yes, 8's attitudes are also like linebackers.

Relieved, Dud thanks the veteran for the crash course. O'Neil pats Dud on the back and they jog towards Coach Wylie.

Later, the team scrimmages and Austin serves as the referee. The pace is relentless as they sprint up and down the field. But skills are improving and play looks surprisingly fluid.

After Turk makes a long run chased by Farish, Austin is bent over, huffing from trying to keep up. Grinning, Rudy pats his back consolingly as he lifts the whistle from Austin's neck and drapes it around his own.

INT. ST GERMAIN RESTAURANT - COAT ROOM - DAY

Having completed morning practice Wylie and Austin are tucked away in the St. Germain restaurant coat room to decide who makes the travel team. Austin finishes reading off his picks for the 23-man list.

AUSTIN
...the Slaters, Charlie Roe, John O'Neil, and Alan Valentine.

WYLIE (UPSET)
Eh? Who's Valentine? And what about Caesar Mannelli and that 220-yard dash star, Turkington?

Austin is taken aback by Wylie's agitation.

AUSTIN
What's eating you, Big Jim? Last time I saw your feathers ruffled was... well must'a been the USA - All Blacks game in '13.

Wylie sighs and tells Austin he can't go to Paris with the team because of an immigration issue. Austin is shocked and upset. Wylie assures him there's nothing to be done and checks the time on his watch.

WYLIE

Gotta finalize the list, Charlie. Why do you want to cut Mannelli?

AUSTIN

Don't want to. But Valentine's been playin' all year at Oxford. He's big enough to be a backup prop. Swarthmore football 210 pounder. Mannelli's a big kid. But he lacks experience, and we're low on that.

WYLIE

You know best, coach. It's killing me I can't go. And now you're stuck without a pack coach.

AUSTIN

Well, Valentine already said he'd assist. But he's only played a year. Maybe I'll write him, see

if he can find us an
English coach. I want a
real pack expert, like
you.

Austin bites his cigar so he can put his arm around Big Jim, a bottle of Coke occupying his other hand.

WYLIE
I appreciate that, Charlie.
She'll be right.

Austin and Wylie depart for the banquet room where the team is eating lunch.

INT. ST GERMAIN RESTAURANT - DAY

Lunch at the St. Germain restaurant has wrapped up. Austin, Rudy, Wylie, and the rest of the prospective team stand in the lobby as Austin pins the final travel team roster up on an easel and turns around. He thanks everyone for coming out and contributing, whether or not they made the team.

Then Austin steps aside to make the list visible. Moans and excited mumbling fill the lobby. Turk reads the list twice and is devastated not to find his name.

AUSTIN
You boys not picked can
go. Thank you for tryin'
out. But you 23 selected,

get ready to puke what you just ate.

Turk and Caesar console one another.

Austin has moved to the corner of the lobby and is talking with some players. He looks disbelieving and exasperated. He asks for everyone's attention again.

AUSTIN

Tilden here can't make the trip for medical reasons. And Mehan can't get away from his job.

RUDY (SARCASTICALLY)

Can't get away from his job?

Several players laugh.

AUSTIN

Quiet! Mannelli. Turkington. You've got a boat to catch if you can figure this sport out in the next few months.

Turk's face lights up.

TURK

Can't believe it! We're
going to--

Caesar smiles broadly and lifts Turk off the ground in a giant bear hug.

TURK (CONT'D)
--Pari-OHHWFF!

INT. ST FRANCIS HOTEL - DAY

SERIES OF SHOTS: The team practices and conditions hard in the San Francisco area.

TITLE OVER: March 6, 1924 - Two months later

Team USA hosts a luncheon in the hotel's formal dining room. Rugby players sit among the business men and ladies. A jazz trio plays in the background. Affable O'Neil is engaged in animated conversation with a WELL-DRESSED MAN and a WEALTHY LOOKING LADY. Louise, dressed in more humble but still fashionable clothes, sits proudly between her two sons.

Rudy steps to the podium and asks for everyone's attention. The music and conversations fade out. A flashbulb snaps.

RUDY
Among you are some of
the finest athletes
California has to offer. In
addition to a few

experienced ruggers, you are sitting with basketball, baseball, football, and track stars. Though we have different backgrounds, we've all come together and, I might add, worked our tails off in the past few months to become a cohesive team. Friends, we're absolutely chomping at the bit to represent America in the upcoming Games.

He raises his glass. The audience applauds.

RUDY

But we need your help to get there. We can *all* take part in representing America. Together, we can make our nation proud. To the Gold!

Glasses lift.

CROWD

To the Gold! (Applause.)

RUDY

No, seriously, to the
gold. We need your
donations, or we don't
go.

Laughter dissolves into the din of many conversations. A few players circulate pledge pads and pencils around the tables.

Later, Austin scrutinizes the pads, saying he thinks they have enough with O'Neil's contribution. Rudy peers over Austin's shoulder and his eyes widen.

RUDY
That's some heavy sugar!

INT. SCHOLZ LAW OFFICES - DAY

In a flurry of activity, Rudy collects papers into a folder and quickly signs a letter presented by his SECRETARY.

RUDY
Bill Chritton will be your
primary point of contact
for my cases.

SECRETARY
Yes, Mr. Scholz.

RUDY
I want nothing hanging.
No one left wondering
what happened.

SECRETARY (NODDING)
Understood, Mr. Scholz. Also, some of your clients are here without appointments. They seem concerned.

Just then, an AGITATED OLD MAN walks in.

OLD MAN
What the hell is this, Scholz? A game comes up and you just drop everything and take off?

Rudy is speechless, taken completely off-guard. Then the man's face changes, breaking into a broad smile. He beckons forward a large cake with "Good Luck Rudy!" written across the top in red, white, and blue icing.

OLD MAN (WINKING)
Gotcha. April Fools!

Other clients emerge with napkins and forks, also smiling, and place them on Rudy's desk. Rudy, recovering from the shock, shakes hands with the man.

OLD MAN
We just wanted to come by to wish you bon voyage! San Franciscans are a tough lot. Heck, we

survived the fire. I think
we can manage, even if
the best damn lawyer in
town leaves for the
Olympics!

The group takes turns shaking hands with Rudy and they begin passing out pieces of cake.

EXT. 16TH ST STATION - DAY

TITLE OVER: April 2, 1924 - Oakland, California

Steam sprays on the tracks as a band plays out a farewell medley. Caesar stands on the platform with his parents. His dad is big, though not as big as him, and his mother is short and plump. Together they are hugging and kissing him repeatedly and speaking loudly in Italian.

Marguerite, her husband ALBERT MESSENGER, their THREE CHILDREN, and Louise say goodbye to Colby and Norman. Louise, on tiptoe, kisses their cheeks.

Turk stands alone on the platform, glancing around and waiting. Elaine materializes out of the crowd. Turk walks quickly over to her.

TURK
You made it!

He hugs Elaine. Her expression is reserved.

TURK

I've been doing some
thinking, and I wanted
you to know... I'm really
gonna miss you.

Elaine's face softens.

ELAINE
I've already had to miss
you for months. What
you did really hurt, Ed.

Turk looks away and rubs his eyes.

TURK
I know, I know, I'm
sorry. I just can't have
my head and my body on
opposite sides of the
Atlantic. I've got to stay
focused.

Several beautiful YOUNG LADIES pass close by and Turk's eyes flick over to them. The train's whistle screeches out. The CONDUCTOR checks his pocket watch.

CONDUCTOR
All aboard!

ELAINE (COOLLY)
Best of luck to you and
the team. I hope all your

hard work and *focus* pay
off in Paris.

Turk glances toward the other players all beginning to board the train and tells Elaine to hang on. He digs around in his pocket and produces Elaine's engagement ring, the same one she previously gave back, holding it out in his palm.

TURK
I was wondering if you'd
like to hold onto this. For
safekeeping?

O'Neil, squeezing through, notices Turk offering the ring to Elaine before he boards. Elaine looks at it for a moment, sighs, and shakes her head.

ELAINE
No. You took it, you
keep it.

The Overland Limited slowly surges forward. The dedicated railroad car is splashed with decorations and painted signs reading "OLYMPIC RUGBY TEAM," "PARIS, OR BUST!" and "ONLY 6000 MILES TO GO!"

Players' faces appear in the windows as the rugby car lurches into motion. Colby makes eye contact with Louise and she waves. As the train gains speed, she presses her hands to her mouth. Her smile melts away into a look of deep concern and her eyes become glassy.

INT. RUGBY CAR - DAY

The team is gathered on the train. Austin reveals the upcoming English exhibition games versus Devonport Services and Harlequins. He emphasizes that conditioning is crucial. There's no time for distractions, especially of the late-night variety, with their two-a-day workout schedule. Austin moves on to the captaincy.

AUSTIN
Time to elect captains.
Half you starters are new
to rugby. We need strong
leaders to have a chance.

Rudy clearly thinks he's a viable candidate. He has continued to assist Austin throughout the formation of the team, and helps especially now that Austin's between assistant coaches. Rudy hands out pencils and paper scraps for the team to vote. They choose Colby, who weakly suggests someone else might make a better captain before he gives in to the wishes of the team. Rudy is disappointed but hopes for the vice captaincy.

TURK (ASIDE)
Why'd they vote for
Slater? Shouldn't you be
captain, Rudy?

RUDY
There's enough old guys
who remember what a

force Colby was years
ago.

5'8" veteran back, CHARLIE ROE, helps Rudy pass out pencils and paper scraps for the vice captain vote. As he collects written votes, he slyly stuffs them in his left pocket, then hands dummy votes from his right pocket to Austin for counting. Roe is elected vice captain. Rudy is devastated.

INT./EXT. CHICAGO RAIL YARD - DAY

Camaraderie otherwise grows as the team approaches Chicago. The pack, sitting together in a rear car, talk animatedly about the city.

DUD

I'm tellin' you guys,
Chicago is the perfect
town.

A stream of backs pours through the train and past the pack, confusing the pack members. The train slows for its arrival at Union Station. The pack watches as the backs jump off near the rear of the train and jog alongside before racing each other to the front.

Turk just barely scrapes out a win over Hyland. They're followed by Lefty and another wing, GEORGE DIXON, a recent graduate of Cal. Reaching a car near the front of the train, the backs hop on. Austin is snoring in his corner of the main rugby car. Rudy is too sullen to join.

Conductor tries to tell the rugby guys to stop but they just smile and blow past to race again.

Having watched the process once, Farish gets up to go with the backs. Other pack members ask what he's doing, joining the backs, especially in a speed contest. Jaws drop as they watch Farish beat out Dixon, coming in neck and neck with Rogers and only behind Turk and Hyland.

Later, the train pulls into the station, waking Austin up. He groggily tells the team to get ready for practice and to be prepared to sweat. Blinking his bleary eyes, he squints at his backs, finally noticing they're already sweaty and panting. Austin gives them a quizzical look.

SERIES OF SHOTS:

-The team steps off the train

-They run through an abbreviated practice

-The train moves again

-Colby watches the landscape pass through his window

-The team is awe-struck at a stop in Niagara Falls

EXT. NEW YORK - PARK AVENUE HOTEL - DAY

TITLE OVER: April 8, 1924 - Park Ave. Hotel - New York City

The team arrives, lugging heavy bags. Rudy stays detached. A note left at the front desk by the AOA makes Austin angry. "Please remind your Paris-bound team to take their beatings like gentlemen."

EXT. HUDSON RIVER PIER - DAY

The team loads onto a passenger luxury liner. The dock is crowded and a band plays. A pier-level placard says "SS America" and "Good luck, U.S. Rugby Team!" A single-file line of players moves up and onto the ship. Turk looks down from the gangway at The Hudson River.

TURK
Didn't this ship sink once?

ROE
Dry up, Ed. No pun.

Team members enjoy the views from the deck. Turk notices a number of attractive young women still waiting to board. He waves, flashes his most dashing smile, and nudges Caesar. Caesar blushes instantly.

SERIES OF SHOTS:

-SS America sails

-Rudy plays shuffleboard with some ladies

-Farish does push-ups alone, in a crew-only area of the deck

-Some team members chat in the dining room

Turk and two ladies, named FRANCESCA and PETE, sit at the bar. O’Neil walks by and slaps Turk upside the head without looking or missing a beat. Turk jolts up with an angry face. He turns to see O’Neil walking away.

INT. STATEROOM - DAY

Rudy’s wind-up alarm sounds in his room on the ship, showing it's 6:30 AM. Without looking, Rudy flicks the catch. He lifts his rumpled head and looks at his practice gear hanging in the closet. His running shoes are on the closet floor next to an open duffel with O’Neil stenciled on its side. Rudy resignedly drops his face back into the pillow.

EXT. SS AMERICA - DECK - DAY

Austin is on the deck conducting practice. He distractedly checks his watch and shakes his head.

AUSTIN (YELLING)
O'Neil! Where's your roommate?

Later, the team is running laps around the rolling deck. Rudy finally arrives. Austin notices but says nothing. Coastal England is visible on the horizon.

A small group of players jogs by. Caesar asks what part of England that is. Farish, in his oddly formal manner, answers that it's Plymouth.

LINGERING SHOT OF PLYMOUTH. 1924 FADES INTO 1890.

BEGIN MONTAGE: BOY'S CHILDHOOD

ELEVEN-YEAR-OLD BOY'S 1ST PERSON PERSPECTIVE.

EXT. CIRCUS GROUNDS - DAY

TITLE OVER: 1890 - Somewhere in England

INT. BIG TOP - DAY

-A boy moves past strange circus workers practicing their acts; he turns left between cages containing prowling tigers and glaring apes; the band practices a piece by Gustav Peter on the other side of the big top.

-A lion roars, people scream, a whip cracks; the boy runs *towards* the commotion, getting knocked against a cage by a fleeing circus worker.

-Determined, the boy continues before turning right toward the lion cage and abruptly running into the spots of a CLOWN.

-Clown turns and restrains the boy who struggles to get past, shouting a muted, "Daaaad!" The boy's father has been mauled.

INT. MAKEUP TENT - NIGHT

-The boy's MUM towers over him and Clown from her riser; muted dialogue: Clown pleads as Mum's expression becomes sour; Mum shakes her head and closes her eyes as she walks away from the dimly lit tent; alarmed, the boy yells, "Mum?!"

INT. CIRCUS 2 - BIG TOP TENT - DAY

TITLE OVER: Six months later

-The boy bounces bareback at different circus locations, day after day, until the day he falls. (See Apx. B shot.)

INT. MEDIC TENT - NIGHT

-The boy is on a gurney next to the RINGMASTER and a slimy looking MEDIC; Medic grabs the boy's arm, which is in a cast, and holds it out for Ringmaster to inspect; Ringmaster looks disgusted and flips his wrist; the boy finally cries.

EXT. FEGAN'S HOME - DAY

-The boy stands outside a building; the boy looks up at the sign: "Fegan's Home for Boys".

INT. FEGAN'S HOME - DAY

-Inside an orphanage room packed with bunk beds, the boy stares at one small window letting sunlight in.

END MONTAGE.

EXT. DOCKYARD - DAY

OPEN ON A SHOT OF PHIL LEWIS. ALAN VALENTINE IS AT HIS LEFT. JAMES PETERS IS VISIBLE IN THE BACKGROUND.

PHIL LEWIS, a stocky, hard looking Englishman in his forties, checks his pocket watch. He comments that the Americans' ship should be arriving any minute. Lewis and Valentine discuss the upcoming exhibition match.

JAMES PETERS, a black Englishman, is working as a carpenter on an exterior doorway. He wears a printer's hat made of newspaper that doesn't quite cover his graying hair. Peters perks up at the mention of rugby.

ALAN VALENTINE, a gregarious and brawny American from Long Island, notices. Greeting Peters, Valentine comments on the carpenter's work and asks if he's a rugby fan.

PETERS
I am, or was. You look to
be a 6?

Phil Lewis's eyebrow raises as he turns his entire body to overcome his bull neck.

VALENTINE (SMILING)
Indeed. Normally I'm a flanker, but I'll be playing 5 at the Olympics. The Americans are short on locks. Not to worry, I hear our 4 is enormous. Haven't met the chaps as I've been at Oxford all year. Shame on me.

With that, Valentine walks towards Peters with his hand outstretched and introduces himself. Peters gingerly pulls his right glove off and shakes.

PETERS
James Peters. Pleasure.

Lewis gruffly asks Peters if he played rugby.

PETERS
Saw some action at 10. You, Mr..?

LEWIS (CONSPIRATORIALLY)
Lewis. Phil Lewis. 15.

They all laugh.

LEWIS

I promised this yank I'd
coach their pack from
here till the Olympics.

Valentine invites Peters to the exhibition game and Peters promises to think about it, saying it's been quite a while since he watched a rugby match.

EXT. RECTORY FIELD - DAY

Six thousand spectators attend the game. The Devonport Services RFC logo is displayed on boundary flags.

RUDY
Criminy! You'd think a
massive guy like
Mannelli could stand his
ground. The French'll eat
us alive!

A nearby ENGLISH SPECTATOR agrees.

ENGLISH SPECTATOR
You play for the
Americans?

RUDY
When I'm not getting
punished.

ENGLISH SPECTATOR

You'll be saying
something about the
scrumming form, then?

RUDY
Say something about it?
Look at me, I'm a wing!
Does a forward tell me
how to score?

SERIES OF SHOTS:

-Hyland scores

-Rudy accepts English Spectator's offered flask

-USA loses a scrum though O'Neil wins the hook

-Lefty makes a crushing tackle

RUDY
Not bad for a basketball
guy.

SERIES OF SHOTS:

-USA loses another scrum

-Lewis wanders a few yards out onto the field, yelling instructions to Caesar on his propping form

-Austin tells Lewis to step back off the field

-Peters hesitates before the entry gate at halftime

The English crowd, good sports, embrace Rudy and ask him to teach them his college yells. He's flattered.

MORE SHOTS: Hyland scores again off an interception; Peters hovers near the sidelines; backs, BOB DEVEREAUX and NORMAN CLEAVELAND, are mostly uninvolved on offense for lack of balls won by the pack and delivered by Roe; Lewis introduces Peters to Austin; Caesar demolishes an ENGLISH CENTER; Hyland scores once again off an ugly pass from Farish.

USA wins, and the American veterans calmly shake hands with the Brits while the rugby rookies cheer and dance.

EXT. TWICKENHAM STADIUM - DAY

TITLE OVER: USA vs. Harlequins - Two days later

The Harlequins look hardened, confident and sharp during warm-ups, though generally smaller than the U.S. players. Rudy is dressed-out, ready to play wing.

Kickoff: the action begins. The Quins and fans, alike, are taken aback by the violent, American football-style tackling. Dud and 30-year-old Cornell graduate, ALAN WILLIAMS, sandwich tackle English player J. M. CURRIE and his leg breaks.

Complaints are directed to the Welsh referee ALBERT FREETHY, but he shakes his head. The American football-style tackling is unprecedented in Europe, yet legal. The Quins play on confidently, weathering the violent hits, and start turning the momentum around.

The Americans continue to lose the scrums. Lefty Rogers breaks his nose but refuses to leave the pitch which would leave his team a man down. Austin and an American TRAINER with round spectacles tend to Lefty's nose from the sideline. USA finally wins a scrum but doesn't get far. After Austin yells, Peters gets involved coaching Devereaux. Farish steals a score.

Halftime: the coaches frantically work with their players. O'Neil winces and discreetly pulls up his jersey and looks at his stomach.

2nd half: Though the Americans make the occasional good play, the experienced and well-conditioned Harlequins steadily increase their lead.

SHIFT TO 1ST PERSON COACH'S PERSPECTIVE FROM SIDELINE.

Dixon scores for USA, but it's too little too late.

BEGIN MONTAGE: BOY/MAN THRIVES

BOY/MAN'S 1ST PERSON PERSPECTIVE.

INT./EXT. FEGANS HOME - DAY

-Young boy walks toward bunk room window and sees children running and passing a rugby ball; the boy plays rugby on that field with the same children; the boy is older, captain of the orphanage team playing in front of a small audience.

EXT. PARIS - RUGBY STADIUM - DAY

TITLE OVER: March 22, 1906 - Parc des Princes, Paris

-Now older, the man claims his first international *cap* in front of a large French crowd; the man scores and is mobbed by ecstatic English teammates (see Apx. B shot).

-Scrum half, ADRIAN STOOP, arrives at the celebration, accidentally bumping a larger FRENCH LOCK who pushes Stoop.

STOOP
(Muted) Bugger off,
Frog.

FRENCH LOCK (SNIDELY)
(Muted) Frog? I'm from
Philly.

The match continues.

EXT. WAREHOUSE - DAY

TITLE OVER: September 1906

-The man's FELLOW CONSTRUCTION WORKER tosses down a rope from the warehouse's roof hatch; ominously near the wall-mounted ventilation fan, the man looks up and grabs the descending rope; he begins to attach it to a bundle of two-by-fours; the rope, wrapped around the man's gloved hand and arm, becomes slack and gets caught in the fan; the man is pulled violently; Fellow Worker's face is horrified.

-Newspaper headline reads, "Rugby Star Loses Three Fingers."

INT. HOSPITAL - DAY

-The man is in a hospital bed with his left arm in traction; blood is visible where his fingers are missing.

EXT. PRACTICE FIELD - DAY

-The man walks outside with a heavily bandaged hand; over time, the man's bandage shrinks as he begins to condition and practice rugby again.

EXT. INVERLEITH - RUGBY STADIUM - DAY

TITLE OVER: March 1907 - Inverleith, Scotland

-The man claims his next *cap*, walking onto the sunny pitch in Edinburgh in front of a large crowd; the man delivers a clutch pass to his ENGLISH TEAMMATE who scores; the man runs to congratulate his rugby brother.

END MONTAGE.

INT. LONDON - PRINCESS RESTAURANT - NIGHT

The Harlequins and Americans mingle freely in the restaurant, displaying mutual respect and camaraderie. Rudy is absent. Players merrily recount the game.

Valentine shows up with Lewis and Peters. Peters gravitates towards a dimly lit, quiet corner of the restaurant where Colby and Farish already stand. The WIVES of the English coaches are seated nearby.

Some rowdy players start tossing a rugby ball inside the restaurant. Austin dodges around them. He tips his hat to WIFE 1, then shakes hands with Peters, thanking him for helping out with the backs.

AUSTIN
You gotta come to the Olympics.

Peters is surprised.

AUSTIN
Need you to coach the halfbacks, 'specially fly-half.

PETERS
Devereaux looked chipper today.

AUSTIN
He's a good athlete. But you and I both know

we'll get stomped unless
he gets a crash course.

ACROSS THE ROOM

Jovial QUINS PLAYERS compliment the Americans loudly on their athleticism and guts, some revealing it was the hardest game they ever played. Turk and a girl get handsy at the bar. Valentine walks by.

VALENTINE
I hear you have a nice
girl back home,
Turkington.

TURK (SNIDELY)
Bad time for your
Quaker talk, Val. Jump
back in your oats box.

Turk instantly regrets the insult, even more when he sees Valentine's smile fade. Turk slides from his stool and breaks into a full sprint with Valentine in chase.

THE CORNER

FARISH
What do you think, Mr.
Peters?

PETERS

I'm not sure... it's been
some time since I went
to Paris.

Peters looks pensive. Without warning someone spins a sharp pass intended for Farish, unaware. Just before the ball hits WIFE 2, Peters pulls his hands from his pockets and catches the ball with a smack. The stubs of three missing fingers show on his left hand.

BEGIN FLASHBACK:

BEGIN MONTAGE: TRAUMA RE-VISITATIONS (NOW IN 3RD PERSON)

-Lion mauls father, GEORGE PETERS (black skin).

-Abandonment by mother, HANNAH GOUGH (white skin).

-The boy, James Peters, falls from horse (brown skin).

END MONTAGE.

END FLASHBACK.

THE BAR

Hyland observes to Cleaveland that the coach in the corner is still agile for an old guy and they should get more action if James Peters trains Devereaux. Adrian Stoop turns all the way around from his seat at the bar.

THE CORNER

Stoop uncomfortably greets Peters, asking where he's been. Stoop almost pleads with Peters, emphasizing that he never wanted to take his position.

PETERS
Adrian, I understand.
And I'm impressed
you're still with it at our
age, though not
surprised.

STOOP (RELIEVED)
Well my body's nothing
like it used to be. My, we
had some good times,
didn't we? I'm sure I'll
forgive you for
disappearing... someday.

Being called, Stoop excuses himself.

COLBY
You played with him?

PETERS
I did, Mr. Slater. Adrian
St--

Peters is interrupted by Austin's booming voice.

AUSTIN

Where the hell is Scholz?

NORMAN (MOUTH FULL)
He left early on side-trip to Ireland, coach. Took O'Neil with him.

Peters regains his composure and resumes the conversation.

PETERS
Adrian Stoop is a legend. He taught me and all of England we don't need separate left and right fly-halfs. He conceded the full width of the backfield to me, moving closer to you blokes in the pack. Adrian was my scrum-half.

COLBY
But something went wrong?

PETERS
Please excuse me, Mr. Slater.

COLBY
It's Colby.

Peters departs. Turk blasts back through the room, knocking over a chair with a crash. Colby winces. Valentine is faster than Turk thought he'd be, and closer.

ACROSS THE ROOM

QUINS PLAYER 1 warns American players about the fastest man in rugby, ADOLPHE JAUREGUY.

QUINS PLAYER 1
Mate, if you let them get
the ball to Jaureguy, it's
all over.

His teammates nod earnestly. Lefty absentmindedly touches his healing nose.

LEFTY
I'd like a second opinion.

The group all chuckles together.

EXT. FERRY - DECK - DAY

Caesar and Peters stand at the ferry's rail as it nears the French coast. Turk pukes over the same rail. Caesar appears lost in thought.

CAESAR (PENSIVE)
Haven't seen Europe
since I was a kid.

PETERS

Where were you then?

CAESAR
I was born in Italy,
Coach.

Peters is surprised by the moniker, but pleased.

INT. CUSTOMS AREA - DAY

TITLE OVER: French Customs - Port of Boulogne-sur-Mer

Turk, looking pallid, argues (in English) with a smug CHIEF AGENT from French Customs. The team is seasick and tired. Chief Agent claims the team's papers are not in order and unapologetically tells them they must return across the English Channel. Hyland, beyond frustrated, picks up his bags and begins to move towards the turnstile.

CHIEF AGENT (TO TURK)
Pardonne-moi.

COLBY (ALARMED)
Dick! What are you
doing?

Chief Agent nonchalantly grabs his billy club and raps Hyland's knuckles on the turnstile bar.

HYLAND

HEY! This palooka is
gonna get hit with his
own nut cracker!

Caesar protectively pushes to the front. Chief Agent brandishes his club but Caesar doesn't back away. The Frenchman jabs his stick towards the large American and is promptly disarmed. Meanwhile, Colby pulls Lefty and Turk back and tries to dissipate the situation in a voice too quiet to hear over the shouting that has broken out.

Three more AGENTS with billy clubs come running and Caesar steps towards them, cocking Chief Agent's club like a baseball bat. A LIEUTENANT hurries to a phone, nervously watching the brawl as he dials. Chief Agent takes another club from the adjacent station, sneaks towards Caesar and strikes him firmly on the back of the hamstring. As Caesar falls to the ground, Chief Agent commands his men to disarm him. AGENT 1 grabs for Caesar's club with a single hand. Caesar hangs on, and they both add their second hands to the tug of war. (See pre-storyboard.)

A memory flashes in Colby's mind of skeleton hands gripping rusty guns. Peters notices Colby withdraw from the chaos, hands over ears. AGENT 2 and AGENT 3 cock their batons to subdue Caesar, but think better of it when Valentine, Dud, Norman and Patrick come to his aid.

The team spontaneously follows Hyland who pushes through the rest of the barriers and the door leading outside and onto French soil. They refuse to return to the ship. Caesar rises and returns the club to Chief Agent.

CAESAR
I respect people who work for the good of others, like sculptors and engineers. Your job is meaningful, too, but not the way you do it. For your own power.

Caesar and Chief Agent stare each other down. The Lieutenant hangs up the phone.

LIEUTENANT (IN FRENCH)
Chief, we have orders to let these Americans through.

INT. TRAIN TO PARIS - CORRIDOR - DAY

Colby and Peters sit across from one another (see Apx. C pic) as the train speeds towards Paris. Austin turns to make one more plea as he leaves the compartment.

AUSTIN
Team needs leadership, Colby. If you bolt at the next stop they'll fall apart.

Austin shakes his head as he makes his way forward to the team car just as Farish walks by.

COLBY'S COMPARTMENT

FARISH (POKING HEAD IN)
You want to quit?

COLBY (NOT LOOKING)
Forget it, Farish.

Farish seems oblivious to Colby's upset state. He speaks lightheartedly and with the confidence of an idealist.

FARISH
What's eating you? I know we're a long way from Yolo County, but we've almost made it to Paris. Once we get there, we're gonna need you to be a leader just like your farmhands do back home.

Colby turns to lock eyes with Farish.

COLBY
(beat) Let me know if you want the job of controlling these birds.

FARISH (NONCHALANTLY)

I'm gonna get a Perrier.
Anybody else want one?

Farish leaves.

COLBY
You might as well go
with him. I’m in no
mood to be coached.

PETERS (WITH EMPATHY)
I’ll leave if you prefer.
But I’d rather answer
your question.

Colby looks puzzled.

PETERS
About what happened
with Adrian.

BEGIN FLASHBACK:

EXT. CRYSTAL PALACE - DAY

TITLE OVER: December 8, 1907 - England vs. South Africa pregame

Stoop looks up warily at the HEAD COACH who is walking across the pitch with a COMMISSIONER. Then he looks at Peters, positioned ten yards away and wearing the same white jersey. Peters shrugs.

HEAD COACH
Hold up, Adrian.

Head Coach yells at an assistant to warm up RAPHAEL JAGO, who will be playing 9. Stoop asks what he's done wrong. Head Coach says nothing; Stoop is moving to 10.

STOOP
10? What about Jim?

HEAD COACH
Peters is out.

STOOP
But he’s the best fly-half
in England. Better than
me, anyway.

HEAD COACH
I won't argue with that.

Head Coach explains that the Boks won't come out with Peters on the pitch. Stoop is angry and incredulous. Head Coach says to ask the commissioner about it. Commissioner explains that the players from South Africa will not come out as long as there’s a black person, or "a savage" to use their term, on the pitch.

SERIES OF SHOTS:

-Peters on the bench

-Kick off with Stoop playing fly-half

-Peters watches Stoop take pass after pass from Jago

Agitated, Peters retreats to the locker room. He doesn't look back though one of his teammates calls after him.

INT. CRYSTAL PALACE - LOCKER ROOM - DAY

Peters stands in front of a mirror, heaving with emotion. After a searching gaze, he takes a sharp breath, grips the collar of his rugby jersey, and screams as if releasing all the pain he's had to bear since he was eleven. Then Peters head butts his reflection and the mirror shatters.

END FLASHBACK.

COLBY
Where did you go after
that game?

PETERS
I disappeared... during
the game. I left that
stadium and went
straight to hell, my own
personalized hell.

Peters explains that his isolation allowed him to stay angry. That leaving his rugby family, his only family, was the worst mistake he ever made. Colby asks about Peters' biological family, learning about the death of Peters' father and the abandonment by his mother. Colby recounts his own father's death. Peters shows empathy for Colby's loss.

PETERS
So now you're looking for a way out. (beat) Don’t do it. Find a way to connect with people, to participate in the world. You're fighting for your life... fighting to have a life. Don’t end up like me. Stay on the train.

COLBY
(beat) How'd you climb out of hell?

PETERS
A chap named Valentine invited me to a rugby game. My climb started when I decided to go.

EXT. GARE SAINT LAZAR - DAY

Team USA is on the platform, exhausted, and looking around with confused expressions.

After hours of waiting, Colby rubs his eyes in the glare of the sinking sun. Austin argues irrationally with some cabbies about getting a bus for the team. The players are sitting on their gear, fatigued.

A friendly AMERICAN REPORTER approaches Turk and describes the way to the team's hotel. He knows where it is because he interviewed the soccer team there.

TURK

Thanks. But how will we fit twenty of us and our gear in a cab?

Colby, fed up, hoists a large gear bag over his shoulder and grabs his suitcase with his other hand. He begins walking in the direction American Reporter indicated.

AMERICAN REPORTER

Good question. Where are you going?

TURK

I think we're walking.

AMERICAN REPORTER

Really? It's over four miles!

The team slowly follows Colby, moving west onto Rue Saint Lazar. Turk and American Reporter rush through detailed directions to the hotel. Turk trots to the front.

EXT. HOTEL EXELMANS - EVENING

SERIES OF SHOTS:

-Colby immediately goes to his room upon arrival

-The guys horse around, making long passes in and across the street (see pre-storyboard)

-They lose some balls and have to hoist and lower one another up to balconies and down into window wells

The skinny desk clerk, who doubles as a WAITER, hands Roe an envelope from the French Olympic Committee. It contains apparent punishments for the incident in Boulogne, including a change of practice field and cancelled warm up games. The coaches arrive by cab and Roe shows them the letter. Norman returns from checking out the new practice field.

NORMAN
It's a beaut.

PETERS
So, it's a nice field, then?

NORMAN
Not exactly.

EXT. VACANT LOT - DAY

The next morning, the team arrives at their practice field, which is more of a bumpy vacant lot littered with broken bricks and trash. Austin is furious.

Colby walks the perimeter, getting away from the upset chatter. Lewis sends Dud jogging back to the hotel for the missing second bag of balls. Norman, Cleaveland, and Lefty knock on doors, attempting to borrow some rakes.

A few LOCAL BOYS who happen to have an American football spot Dud. BOY 2 pleads with him to throw them a pass, American style. Dud plays along and throws a long bomb to BOY 1. It rockets between his hands and smashes a parked car's windshield (see Apx. C pics) instead.

Finishing his perimeter walk, Colby shakes his head at the chaos, turns and walks the other direction. Patrick goes over to inspect the car, plucking glass from the windshield while laughing. An old man (VIEIL HOMME) emerges from his front door and takes Patrick for a thief. The man cracks Patrick on the upper back with his cane, yelling.

VIEIL HOMME

Voleur!

PATRICK

Hey! Ow! Watch it, Bub!
Why'd you brain me?

The team, Boy 1 and Boy 2 fall over with laughter.

INT. HOTEL DINING ROOM - DAY

The team quietly has tea together. A table with a display of hard bread and celery is visible near the pot. Rudy enters in a business suit. With him is O'Neil.

TURK
Well look what the cat dragged in.

CAESAR
Glad you gals could make it.

O'NEIL
Why you guys dressed out?

TURK (QUIETLY)
Coach wants a second practice today...

RUDY (ADOPTS LOUD IRISH ACCENT)
The side trip to Ireland 'twas splendid, a good craic...

Rudy is smiling, buoyant.

RUDY
Except for a minor setback when O'Neil got an emergency appendectomy. We

didn’t miss anything, did
we?

The others stare blankly at him, then gawk at O'Neil. O'Neil shrugs happily, feeling fine.

RUDY (IMPATIENT)
Who died?

Turk taps the front page of a nearby newspaper laid out on the table, indicating an article about the Americans' forced entry onto French soil in which the Americans are referred to as "street fighters and barroom brawlers."

Rudy asks where Colby is and, to his surprise, Caesar says he's out in the lobby about to give an interview.

INT. HOTEL LOBBY - DAY

Colby walks into the lobby biting a hard roll. He looks up, not expecting journalists yet, and almost chokes. The Excelsior's reporter, 42-year-old ANDRE GLARNER, beckons his RUNNER towards the front.

Colby meekly introduces himself and asks for questions, but the FRENCH REPORTERS all talk at once threatening to overwhelm him. He begins to talk about the assembly of Team USA but REPORTER 2 interrupts, asking about the Boulogne melee. Colby begins to answer and REPORTER 3 interrupts, asking about USA abandoning France post WWI.

COLBY

That's enough! The Olympic Games are supposed to be about unity, about nations coming together, and here you are trying to provoke me with questions about the war. We've received dismissive, even hostile treatment from the get-go. First you goad us into bringing a team for a sport we don't play. Then, when we do assemble one and travel 6,000 miles to be here, you turn us away at Boulogne.

The players start to collect behind Colby. He punctuates each word with the hard roll still in his hand.

COLBY (LOUDER)
You take away the warm up games we desperately need while we starve by way of your... bird food...

Colby looks at the roll, then suddenly throws it at the wall. The loud pop makes Reporter 3 jump.

COLBY

... you give us a tiny lot full of bricks and glass as a practice pitch!

Teammates start to audibly validate Colby.

COLBY

Now, you call us abandoners when 100,000 Americans gave their lives in the war to protect the French people? My friends DIED!

Colby breathes heavily. Norman quickly wipes a tear escaping down his cheek. Glarner tears a sheet from a notepad, handing it to Runner who exits. Teammates yell in support.

Colby marches out the front door and his team follows. A WELL-DRESSED FRENCHMAN entering pauses to avoid collision.

EXT. RUE CHANEZ - DAY

Led by Colby, the team jogs confidently in two columns down Rue Chanez. Colby stops the line of ruggers, looking back to summon Turk who asks a FRIENDLY POLICEMAN for directions.

They pass practice balls between the columns. Some locals across the street point at them and yell with disdain. A thin MAN WATERING a balcony plant spits down at the Americans.

EXT. COLOMBES STADIUM - DAY

Later, the team arrives at the stadium. Colby lifts the heavy lock and large steel chain wrapped around the metal gate, then drops it with a loud clank.

TURK

Wait! I've got an idea.
Caesar!

EXT. ALLEY - DAY

Turk beckons with a jerk of his head, then backtracks into the nearest alley, followed by Caesar. They arrive at the back of a house, enter the gate, and tiptoe through the garden to grab a ladder hanging from the side of a free-standing garage.

Tiptoeing back through the garden, Caesar accidentally crushes a flower. Making a *yikes* face, he mouths sorry in the direction of the house.

EXT. COLOMBES STADIUM - DAY

As they return to the stadium, the group of players makes way for the ladder.

ROE (GRINNING)

I know you're new,
Turk, but carrying
weight is the job of the
pack.

Farish offers to take over at the front of the ladder.

ROE (SHAKING HIS HEAD)
I was kidding, Farish.
Geez.

Turk and Caesar prop the ladder against the gate and hold it as the team, led by Colby, climbs over and into the stadium.

SERIES OF SHOTS:

-Three cabs depart Hotel Exelmans in succession, containing Andre Glarner, competing reporters and coaches

-Glarner's cab stops periodically and he talks to pointing pedestrians

-Practice is in full swing in the stadium; the team revels in the pristine field, showing off their speed and endurance now that they finally have room to run

-Three cabs arrive at the stadium in succession

-Turk is attempting to translate as Austin argues with several low-level officials and groundskeepers

-Glarner, Reporter 2 and Reporter 3 crowd around the gate taking notes while PHOTOGRAPHER 1 and PHOTOGRAPHER 2 snap photos through the bars

-Peters shades his eyes with both hands. As he watches the backs run flowing lines while Austin bellows at an OBJECTING OFFICIAL, Peters cracks a broad smile

INT. HOTEL DINING ROOM - NIGHT

The team is eating dinner. Players dig in enthusiastically to the much-improved food. Waiter brings in a fresh plate of steaming beef and players grin, nudging each other in happy anticipation.

O'NEIL
Hey Bub! Merci for the meat!

WAITER (GRINNING)
Je vous en prie, Monsieur.

Austin chuckles and turns back to Rudy, Colby, and Peters sitting at his table.

AUSTIN
Looks like stirrin' the pot worked...

COLBY (MOUTH FULL)
Hmm?

AUSTIN (SMIRKING)
Never mind. Remember,
France versus Romania
tomorrow. 2 PM sharp.

COLBY (SWALLOWING)
We'll be there, coach.

EXT. COLOMBES STADIUM - PLAYING FIELD - DAY

TITLE OVER: May 4th, 1924 - Opening match of the Olympics: France vs. Romania

Adolphe Jaureguy and the rest of the French are warming up on the field. Jaureguy runs with the ball, dodging and cutting. The American team, dressed in gentlemanly attire, makes its way into the stadium.

Pierre takes his place high above the field in his VIP box. He looks out proudly across the crowd of around 14,000. Carrying sausage sandwiches, O'Neil and Norman head to the section where their teammates are seated.

NORMAN
Wow. That Jaureguy's
reputation is no joke,
he's fast.

As they climb the stands, Norman and O'Neil are jostled rudely by a passing group of ROUGH FRENCH SPECTATORS. O'Neil winces and drops a hand to his surgery site.

ROUGH SPECTATOR 1 (IN FRENCH)
American scum! Watch what happens today. It will be your turn next!

Norman has to keep O'Neil from going after the man. The Frenchmen laugh and make obscene gestures.

VALENTINE
We're not in England anymore, gentlemen.

Later, the game is in full swing and the Romanians are being throttled. One Romanian player makes a hopeful run with the ball when MARCEL LUBIN, a large, severe-looking French player with hair groomed to be rigidly vertical, pushes him out of bounds and over the bench. O'Neil winces and leans towards Colby who is watching stoically next to him.

O'NEIL
Poor bastards. Rudy told me they just got off the train from Bucharest this morning.

O'Neil notices Colby kneading his thumb distractedly.

O'NEIL
Something wrong with your hand?

COLBY

Jammed it; it's nothing.

Jaureguy deftly evades three Romanians in a row and slows to a jog as he scores the try. Palms up, he shrugs as if waiting for a response and the crowd goes wild.

ERIC LIDDELL, the Scottish rugby star and Olympic sprinter, climbs up the stands extending his hand to Norman.

LIDDELL

Pardon my interruption, gentlemen. Eric Liddell. I'm hoping to meet Mr. Scholz.

Norman and O'Neil stand to shake hands with Liddell, introducing themselves and sharing their position numbers. Liddell says he plays wing at home but is at the Olympics for sprinting.

A ROMANIAN LOCK is tackled. The French recover the ball in the ruck and pass it off to Jaureguy who scores again with ease. After touching the ball to the grass, he stands erect miming a symphonic conductor before taking numerous bows. The French fans laugh heartily. Those near the Americans taunt them more. Liddell, Norman and O'Neil look on sadly.

O'NEIL (POINTING)

That's Scholz, the only one of us shorter than me.

LIDDELL
Thank you, gentlemen.
Enjoy.

Liddell moves down a few rows and over towards Rudy.

LIDDELL
Good afternoon. My name is Eric Liddell. I'm looking forward to seeing you on the track, Mr. Scholz.

RUDY (STANDING TO SHAKE)
Oh. Hi. Rudy Scholz. It's nice to meet you, Eric. But you won't find me on the track, I only sprint on the grass.

LIDDELL
My apologies. I mistook you for Jackson Scholz. It's a pleasure to meet you, Rudy, nonetheless.

RUDY
Don't worry about it. Pleasure's mine.

Liddell and Rudy chat. A ROMANIAN CENTER attempts to tackle thick-necked flanker and French captain, RENE LASSERRE. Lasserre turns his rugged face before employing a stiff-arm and Romanian Center falls to the dirt with a bloody nose. As the crowd grows uglier, Pierre looks down at the display, puzzled, as if he doesn't understand what's happening.

CAESAR
So, we play these guys, the Romanians, next week?

RUDY
Yep.

CAESAR
Hope they're healed up by then.

Later, the match is over. On the scoreboard: France 67 Roumanie 3. The crowd chants "JAUR-EY-GUY, JAUR-EY-GUY!" French fans continue to mock and jeer as the Americans hurry to get out. Drunk spectators drop things on them from above as they leave. Glarner interviews Jaureguy on the pitch.

JAUREGUY (IN FRENCH)
You've essentially watched the gold match. I'm going to the Riviera; my work is done in these Olympics.

INT. MUHR'S OFFICE - DAY

TITLE OVER: Two days later

AUSTIN
... gotta have a ref who's impartial. Albert Freethy or we don't play. Also, we want our own film crew, startin' with the USA-Romania game.

Turk translates rapidly.

MUHR (IN FRENCH)
I'm sorry. That is impossible as it would violate the exclusivity clause of the Olympic committee's contract with our official filming company.

Turk begins to translate Muhr's response, then spots a paper on the desk with the article quoting Jaureguy. Aghast, Turk explains to Austin that Jaureguy has left for vacation and won't compete against the Americans.

AUSTIN
Unnn-bee-lievable! Field's so tilted French players are goin' on vacation! I don't care if you French are annoyed. We're here. We're valid. Plus, where I'm from you

get to watch your own
films.

Peters, leaning in the doorway, speaks up.

PETERS
I believe this gentleman
is from Philadelphia.

Muhr, caught off guard, turns to see the quiet middle-aged James Peters standing in his office doorway. Recognizing his old opponent from decades earlier he slowly scoots his chair back and stands.

MUHR (AMERICAN ENGLISH)
Jim? What happened to
you? We thought you
died...

Austin and Turk look at each other and shrug. Peters holds out his hand as Muhr approaches. Muhr ignores the gesture and gives Peters a heartfelt hug. Austin lights a cigar.

MUHR
For friends of this legend
I suppose I will make an
exception. Mr. Austin,
you may hire yourself a
film crew. But only one
camera, off the field.

AUSTIN (PUFFING SMOKE)

(beat) One camera, *on* the field.

MUHR (SURRENDERING)
D'accord.

EXT. COLOMBES STADIUM - PLAYING FIELD - DAY

TITLE OVER: May 11, 1924 - USA vs. Romania

A crowd of 6,000 attends the game. Caesar powers over a ROMANIAN FLANKER to score. French spectators boo. The French team watches from the stands, dressed like gentleman in sharp sweaters. Jaureguy is conspicuously absent. Among the French players are Lubin and scrum-half, CLEMENT DUPONT. Dupont turns towards his large teammate.

DUPONT (IN FRENCH)
Ugh! Look how they butcher our sport! The Americans are arrogant, always doing things *their* way.

LUBIN (SNEERING IN FRENCH)
Yes, and I despise their way. I lost much to the Germans during the Great War: my friends, my own eye. (beat) Now Germany is like a

dangerous dog with
America as its negligent
keeper.

Roe rolls the ball into a U.S. scrum. Williams, playing hooker for the injured O'Neil, wins the ball. But, because of their loose formation and arched backs, the U.S. is pushed. The relative inexperience of Caesar and Dud on the loose head side of the scrum is apparent, allowing Romania to take possession away. Austin waves a PORTLY CAMERAMAN over, points at the scrum using his arms to show the perspective he wants.

Despite scrumming trouble, Hyland scores four tries, and Patrick three. American art student GIDEON NELSON uses a megaphone to lead the small group of American fans in college cheers. Gideon notices Lucia Garrison Norton and her host, 33-year-old LUELLA MELIUS, cheering for the Americans nearby and approaches them.

GIDEON
Lovely day for a match,
huh? Shame your
boyfriend couldn't make
it.

LUCIA (EYES ROLLING)
He doesn't exist.

GIDEON
My, my, what did he do?

Lucia stifles a grin, entertained by Gideon's brazen wit despite herself.

Back on the field, Colby plays well, especially during his powerful runs and in the line-outs. Turk throws a retaliatory punch at Romanian Lock who elbowed his jaw. Turk gets thrown out and complains.

LEWIS
Pipe down, Turkington!
It doesn't matter who hit
first.

Turk approaches the ref to argue but Norman blocks him.

NORMAN
Ixnay, Turk! In rugby,
NOBODY but the
captain speaks to the ref.

Farish sits on the bench, agitated and fuming. O'Neil sits nearby, pressing on his slow-to-heal incision.

O'NEIL
Take it easy, Farish!
You're a good player.
We'll get our chance.

FARISH
I thought subs weren't
allowed.

O'NEIL (CONFIDENTLY)

We'll get our chance.

The final scoreboard shows Etats Unis 27, Roumanie 3. Turk is excited but Lewis, noticing, shakes his head.

LEWIS

We're doomed.

TURK (TO RUDY)

He's just saying that 'cause I got in trouble.

RUDY

He's saying that because he knows we won on sheer athleticism, and that's not enough to beat skill and experience like the French have.

Rudy and Caesar help an INJURED ROMANIAN PLAYER to the locker room. Pierre remains separated in his elevated box, disturbed by the rudeness of the French crowd.

EXT. COLOMBES STADIUM - TRACK - DAY

After the match, Team USA signs autographs. Most French fans walk by disdainfully, but a few kids and FRENCH GIRLS linger, asking various players to sign. Romanian Center waits in line behind a SKINNY KID to get Patrick’s signature.

PATRICK
Didn't I just run over you?

Romanian Center clearly doesn't understand English. He smiles and offers the paper, holding up three fingers.

HYLAND
Maybe he admired your hat trick? Send him over here next, I got a hat trick... plus one.

GIRL 1 and GIRL 2 try to get Turk's autograph but his mind is clearly elsewhere. He takes Girl 1's spare sheet of paper and pencil and wanders over to a bench where he begins a letter to Elaine. She is confused. Once Girl 1 realizes Turk doesn't intend to return the pencil and paper, she rolls her eyes and walks away.

Luella "you-hoos" team USA and has them assemble for the presentation of her gift. She pulls a Leitz camera from her giant handbag and instructs Lucia to take the picture. As the team assembles, Valentine walks over to Lucia and asks about the two of them. Lucia informs him that Luella's from Wisconsin, spending a year singing for the Paris Opera. Luella's a friend of Lucia's mother and she's hosting the Paris portion of Lucia's trip abroad that is her graduation gift. Rudy overhears this conversation.

RUDY (CHARMINGLY)
You don't say! The Paris Opera? I'm a bit of an

enthusiast myself, got lots of exposure in Bavaria. My dear Luella you must tell me everything about it!

LUELLA (PLEASED)
Why don't you see for yourself, Mr. Scholz? You and a few of these other strapping gentlemen can accompany Lucia to my show tonight.

RUDY
Splendid! You say you're a Smithie, Lucia? Couple of our players graduated from east coast schools, as well. Alan Williams over there went to Cornell. And Alan Valentine here went to...

VALENTINE (CLEARING HIS THROAT)
... Huh? Oh, Swarthmore!

Luella sets herself in the middle of the group of players. Lucia wonders out loud if she'll need a tripod and Valentine eagerly kneels, volunteering his shoulder. They both blush slightly at the physical contact as she bends over to set up her shot.

Luella digs again in her bag and produces her gift to the team: a Golliwog doll she named *Cali* with black-brown skin, bulging eyes, and a grass skirt.

RUDY (IMPATIENT)
Hurry up, Turkington!
Ms. Melius wants us in a
picture with her gag gift.

Fury at the racist joke flashes through Peters' eyes. Lucia is also taken aback. She discards the camera, letting it roll on the grass, and starts angrily towards the doll. Luella, busy charming the players, doesn't notice. Having collected himself, Peters grabs Lucia's arm to stop her and whispers in her ear. Luella prods the players to stand closer and smile wide. After negotiating with Peters, Lucia nods, returns to Valentine and resets the shot.

CAESAR
Who feels awkward?

The players raise their hands, smiling. Lucia snaps it.

Later, Lucia asks Colby to borrow the doll to make some alterations. She eyes Williams' torn jersey.

LUCIA
Alan Williams, might I
have what's left of your
jersey? Alan Valentine,

what do you call that
unfortunate hat?

VALENTINE
This? It's a scrum cap.

LUCIA
Let's have it.

Lucia invites Valentine to come alter Cali with her and he readily agrees. Luella also "yoo-hoos" the French team and gets a picture of them, then heads back to her flat to chaperone Lucia and Valentine.

EXT. OUTSIDE THE HOTEL - EVENING

Rudy and Valentine step out of the hotel lobby, handsomely dressed. Rudy turns down a swig from the flushed, FRIENDLY DOORMAN's flask and they chat about Valentine's time at Swarthmore and his Rhodes scholarship. Then Rudy talks about his father selling his bakery and moving the family to Bavaria when Rudy was six to support his mother's music career. Rudy trails off, then hollers at U.S. soccer player, RAYMOND HORNBERGER, exiting the lobby door.

RUDY (POINTING)
Hey Hornberger. Did
you soccer boys lose a
ball in that bush?

HORNBERGER (OVER HIS SHOULDER)
Nah, that's one of yours.

Looking quizzical, Rudy turns to Valentine and shrugs.

VALENTINE (STEPPING FROM THE CURB)
There's an easy way to check.

Valentine strolls across the street to look. A BURLY FRENCH PEDESTRIAN coming along the sidewalk eyes Rudy's red and white striped sport coat and blue bow tie (see Apx C pic). He starts talking smack in French. Rudy is unafraid, but the Frenchman snickers at his size advantage. Then Valentine arrives directly behind him with the practice ball tucked under his muscular arm. Burly Pedestrian turns, cowers and departs, grumbling. Valentine asks if Doorman would kindly hand off the ball to the next American walking in.

Colby steps out of the lobby, also turning down a swig from Doorman's flask. Rudy teases Colby for holding them up as he steps into the street to hail a cab. A cab stops and Rudy climbs in.

CRACK! A bottle disintegrates against the hotel masonry above Colby's head, causing him to jump violently and gasp. Valentine spots Burly Pedestrian watching from behind a car parked across the street. Valentine feints a step towards him and the Frenchman flees. Colby stands still, eyes closed, breathing heavily. Climbing into the cab Valentine explains to Rudy about the balls lost on arrival at the hotel.

VALENTINE (TURNING HIS HEAD)

Come on, cap. Gonna be
late.

Colby doesn't respond.

RUDY
SLATER! Get in!

Colby's eyes open and he slowly climbs in.

RUDY
Palais Garnier. How do
you tell a guy to *move it*
in French? Pronto!
Schnell!

Doorman, ball under arm, looks at the broken glass he presumably must clean up and shrugs. Turning to the cab of Americans speeding away, he tips his flask in salute before taking another sip.

EXT. PALAIS GARNIER - NIGHT

The cab pulls up to Palais Garnier and the ruggers are impressed by its grand architecture. (See Apx. C pics).

INT. PALAIS GARNIER - NIGHT [CONTINUOUS]

Upon entering the lobby, they remain dumbstruck.

LUELLA'S BOX

Rudy sits next to Lucia already in the front row. Colby sits behind Rudy and Valentine sits behind Lucia. Valentine tries not to openly gawk at Lucia looking particularly glamorous.

Lucia presents Cali to Colby, now modified to be a rugby player with the jersey and scrum cap. She notices the sadness in his eyes; he the kindness in hers. They all agree the doll is much improved.

Rudy asks Lucia why she got so hopping mad about the doll. First in French, then English, an announcer asks that the audience take their seats as the opera will begin in a few minutes. Lucia hurriedly explains that she's no fan of racism, sexism, or any 'ism. Among other things, she's the granddaughter of William Garrison Norton the abolitionist. He once came to Europe for a meeting of abolitionists only to get angry that women weren't allowed to sit on the main floor. In protest, he grabbed another key speaker and retreated to a balcony, much like this one, which was the only place women could sit. Rudy is impressed.

SERIES OF SHOTS:

-Luella and the other OPERA SINGERS perform

-Intermission: Valentine leaves for the restroom

Rudy analyzes the first act with Lucia. She points at the program, asking his opinion on one character's motives. Valentine returns from the restroom, takes his seat and leans forward to see the program. His cheek brushes

Lucia's hair and he pulls back slightly before bashfully looking towards her face.

VALENTINE (CLEARING HIS THROAT)

Rudy, you never finished
telling us about the
Bavarian Opera.

Rudy explains for all how his father loved his mother so much he sold his Chicago bakery. Mr. Scholz then used the money to move his family to Germany to support Mrs. Scholz's budding opera career. Colby frowns.

The opera resumes. Soon, tension rises, dramatic music plays, loud wailing comes from the stage and Gilda, Luella's character, commits suicide.

Colby is welling with emotion. He covers his mouth and pinches his nose, but a sob escapes. Lucia turns to look at him, then turns back around quickly, embarrassed. Colby, unable to contain himself, panics and exits the box. Lucia discreetly glances at Colby again and instead sees the Cali doll wearing the scrum-cap alone in his seat. Lucia gets up to leave, concerned. She mouths, "I'll be back" to Valentine.

EXT. STREETS OF PARIS - NIGHT

Colby busts out the side doors of Palais Garnier. He walks briskly down Place de l'Opera, struggling to avoid pedestrians. Lucia comes through the doors after him.

LUCIA

Colby? Colby!

Lucia's voice morphs into Louise's voice, calling Colby.

BEGIN FLASHBACK pt. 1:

INT. SHATTUCK AVE KITCHEN - NIGHT

LOUISE
Colby? Colby!

14-year-old Colby appears in the kitchen doorway and Louise tells him to fetch his step-father, EDWARD PHILLIPS, for dinner. Colby heads for the staircase (see pre-storyboard).

END FLASHBACK.

COLONNE VENDOME

Colby walks faster as he turns right onto Rue de la Paix. Removing her heels, Lucia hurries after. Colby, distressed, stops in the shadows by Colonne Vendome.

BEGIN FLASHBACK pt. 2:

Louise tells 14-year-old Colby to fetch Ed for dinner.

STAIRCASE

Colby is two thirds of the way up the staircase. The stair creaks and Colby senses something is off.

END FLASHBACK.

A police whistle sounds. An OLDER POLICEMAN yells in French at Colby to leave the restricted area. Colby begins to run, using a lamp post to vault the sharp-posted fence, continuing south. (See Apx. C pics.) Lucia arrives at the north end of the square, just in time to spot Colby leaving the south end of the square. Colby runs along Rue de Castiglione.

MERRY-GO-ROUND

Lucia arrives at the end of Rue de Castiglione, crossing into Jardin des Tuileries. She calls Colby again, then sees the merry-go-round (see Apx. C pic) and approaches.

Lucia spots Colby on the moving ride. She rushes onto it and grabs him by the arm only to discover it's ANOTHER RIDING MAN sitting in the carriage with a KID who looks frightened. Lucia apologizes distractedly and stands straight, neck craned. As the carriage comes around, she spots the real Colby sitting on a nearby bench, his head in his hands.

BEGIN FLASHBACK pt. 3:

The stair creaks and Colby senses something is off.

COLBY (TENTATIVELY)
Ed?

END FLASHBACK.

LUCIA
What happened, Colby?
Are you okay?

Colby doesn't respond.

LUCIA
I can't help unless you
talk to me.

Colby remains silent. Lucia grabs his lapels.

LUCIA
Hey! TALK TO ME!

COLBY (BETWEEN RAGGED BREATHS)
Memories... from when I
was young... can't stop
them.

LUCIA
(beat) What memories?

COLBY
My step-dad. Ed. Not
answering. I knew
something was wrong... I
KNEW something was
wrong!

BEGIN FLASHBACK pt. 4:

The stair creaks and Colby senses something is off.

COLBY (TENTATIVELY)
Ed?

LANDING

Colby approaches Louise and Ed's bedroom, stepping on another creaky floorboard. He pauses, then slowly turns the knob, pushing the door open. CRACK! Ed rushes his suicide and falls to the floor. Colby recoils, shocked, staring through the half-open door at Ed's prone torso. (See pre-storyboard).

LOUISE (ALARMED)
Colby, what was that?
Colby? Colby!

Louise runs upstairs, eyes wild. Paralyzed, Colby watches in horror as she rushes into the bedroom and screams upon seeing Ed Phillips' lifeless body, still gripping a pistol.

END FLASHBACK.

Colby, no longer suppressing his grief, sobs into Lucia's arms. A few tears roll down her cheeks as she holds his head.

INT. HOTEL EXELMANS - DAY

Rudy has film reels and a Keystone projector in his arms (see Apx. C pic) as he walks down the hallway. He pauses at the exercise room, hearing players laughing inside.

TURK
Rudy! Come school us in this pub game! O'Neil said you two picked it up in Ireland.

RUDY
Pitch Penny?

NORMAN (GRINNING)
Or "Pitch Franc."

Roe, picking up his winnings, doesn't laugh.

ROE
You heard the man, Mannelli, it's "Pitch Franc," not "Pitch Fifty-Centimes!"

Rudy tells Turk thanks, but he'll pass, and continues to his hotel room.

SCHOLZ'S HOTEL ROOM

Rudy projects the game film onto a bed sheet and studies it with a pencil and legal pad.

INT. SLATER'S HOTEL ROOM - NIGHT

Colby is sitting at the desk in his room writing in his diary when he's interrupted by an insistent knocking. He opens the door to find Rudy holding a mess of torn out pages from the legal pad, looking frazzled but expectant.

RUDY
We gotta change our scrum.

Stunned, Colby stares at him for a moment, then nods.

COLBY (SUPPRESSING ANNOYANCE)
Show me what you've got.

Rudy thrusts the pages into Colby's arms and helps himself to the desk chair Colby just vacated. Rudy explains he's been watching the game film. He notes that while the smaller Romanian pack was able to push the poorly formed American pack, the French pack made the Romanians look like they were wearing roller skates.

RUDY
Do you think there's any chance we fix the form problem in our scrum?

COLBY
(beat) No. It takes years to develop a good prop who can transfer the full power of his scrum.

Mannelli's only been at it
a few months.

RUDY
Right, what about that
then?

Rudy indicates the pages in Colby's arms, but Colby, now seated on the edge of his bed, clearly can't decipher the jumble of scribbles. Rudy hurriedly digs in his pocket and pulls out a handful of coins. He looks around the room and spots a couple of bottle caps on Colby's dresser and grabs those too. Sliding the diary and a Bible aside, Rudy spreads coins and caps out on the desk and counts.

RUDY (DISTRACTEDLY)
Gimme your change.

Colby digs in his pockets and hands Rudy some change.

RUDY
We've been pushed and
we're gonna get pushed
by the French; you know
it and I know it. What we
need is a way to get the
ball out anyhow.

Rudy arranges a scrum formation, pointing to coins and caps and moving them as he speaks.

RUDY

We can change the scrum to three men in the first row and four in the second row, getting rid of you in the third row. No offense. We need fewer legs for the ball to move through on its way to Roe.

COLBY

I don't know... The balls will come out too hot and unpredictable if I'm not controlling them and feeding them to Charlie.

RUDY

I know it's risky, but at least it's a chance to not go home with silver around our necks.

Colby looks uncertain.

RUDY

Look. I've been a real ass. I resented being left out when you became the captain and Roe became vice-captain. And I left the team to go pout in Ireland rather than dealing with my issues like an adult. Honestly, I was surprised you even let me come in here and talk to you at all.

COLBY

Yeah well. I've not been my best either. I'm trying to climb out of my own personal hell.

Rudy looks quizzical but doesn't interrupt.

COLBY

And you're worth listening to. You're the smartest guy I know.

The compliment stuns Rudy for a moment. There's a long pause. Colby looks away and studies the desk. Rudy clears his throat, trying to gather his thoughts.

RUDY

If we don't change something, we lose for sure. Can't win a rugby game without scoring.

COLBY (PENSIVELY)

And we can't score without possessions. It's

true, we're not getting
many from our scrums.

RUDY
Exactly. The boys trust
you. They'll listen to
you. I'm all-in now,
Colby. I'll follow your
lead, whatever you
decide to recommend to
the coaches.

Colby pauses for a moment, looks up from the desk and nods slowly. Rudy yelps in triumph and claps Colby on the back.

EXT. VACANT LOT - DAY

The team is gathered on the vacant lot. A few new bottles and bits of trash are scattered on the field.

AUSTIN
Norman! Williams!
Gimme an opposing
front row. Turkington!
Get over here.

Turk jogs over, tripping on a bottle.

TURK
You want me to--ow!
You want me to play
prop?

LEWIS (LAUGHING)
Should you want to send Mr. Turkington back to join the other prima donnas, I've still got a few scrums left in me, coach.

Peters tries to soften the blow.

PETERS
Come on, Turk. You're far too refined a fellow for scrumming, much less in the front row.

Austin grants Rudy permission to further instruct the pack on the 3-4 scrum. As they implement it, Rudy stands opposite Austin on the other side of the tunnel, squatting to see what happens to the ball. Colby has been moved to flanker. O'Neil is suspended between his props. The abbreviated scrum comes together with no third row.

Austin rolls the ball into the tunnel. O'Neil winces with pain as he heels it backwards. Farish contains the ball with his right leg.

RUDY
Farish! Don't plug up the--

AUSTIN

Hold on, Scholz. A-side,
don’t push so hard.
These three on B-side
need to seem like eight.
Williams, take over for
O’Neil.

O’NEIL

No, coach, I’m fine.

RUDY

All due respect, Williams
can’t hook like we need
here. The idea’s to have
won balls rocket out the
back of the scrum.

Rudy explains to Farish and the rest that the whole concept of the 3-4 scrum is to let the ball out unfettered. That’s why number 8 has been dropped from the back row.

PATRICK

You mean 8's been
shifted to eliminate my
position.

RUDY

Hang on, Jack. Let's just
try it.

Rudy positions Roe back three yards from the scrum, like a football quarterback in shotgun formation. Rudy gets on

Farish's case for previously stopping the ball. Farish counters he was taught by Coach Wiley to contain balls.

COLBY
Do it Rudy's way now, Slim.

For the next hook, Rudy gets down on his stomach to make sure nobody else steps on the ball. Nobody does and the ball flies out at Rudy. He tries to dodge and gets smacked in the side of the face. Austin turns away to hide a smile, but Roe and the players laugh openly. Rudy fights to keep his cool.

RUDY
Okay, okay. It's working now.

As they continue to practice, Roe is unable to get to the wild balls most of the time. Rudy tries to encourage him, but Roe's frustrated.

ROE
Even if I get to the ball, French flankers like that scar-faced Lasserre will clean my clock!

Rudy asks for live action with full scrums. Austin calls the backs over and uses them to make a full opposing pack. Roe finally fields a ball.

RUDY

Now you've got it!

He's tackled hard by Turk, then harder by Patrick. Picking himself up, he wipes blood from his lip in disgust.

ROE

That's it. This is a stupid idea.

RUDY

Don't give up, Charlie! You can do it.

Roe challenges Rudy to try it himself if it's so doable. Rudy agrees. The first ball causes Rudy to dive and miss. But he gets the second, tossing an inside pass to Farish, who pauses, staring at the ball in his hands.

RUDY

Run!

Before trying again, Austin instructs defending flankers to go full speed, doing everything in their power to stop Rudy. They run it again and Patrick bears down, but the smaller man cuts hard before speeding away. The teammates, except for Roe, whoop and cheer.

ROE (SARCASTIC)

Run, run, as fast as you can, can't catch Scholz, he's the Gingerbread Man.

Numerous teammates chuckle as Rudy jogs back.

AUSTIN (GRINNING)
Hurry up, G-man. Again!

Rudy pauses for a moment, then grins broadly at his new nickname. He looks towards Colby, who nods.

Patrick is irritated by being displaced. Austin notices.

AUSTIN
You played fullback at Stanford?

PATRICK
Yeah.

Roe overhears this and whips his head around.

INT. HOTEL DINING ROOM - EVENING

TITLE OVER: May 13, 1924 - Five days until the final

The team, exhausted from practice, eats dinner at the hotel. Rudy reaches the end of the buffet line and heads for the table where the captains and coaches sit. He pauses, then turns instead towards a table where Turk and some rookies are eating enthusiastically.

At the captains' and coaches' table, Austin warns Colby that the players need to stay inside the hotel. Colby looks up from his meal. Austin stirs his food distractedly.

AUSTIN
Need to pick the final
fifteen.

He tells the table to meet in his room in one hour for final selections, adding that not everyone's going to like the results. Roe looks suspiciously at Austin, then over at Patrick. The group continues to eat. Roe slips over to Patrick's table and whispers in his ear.

ROE
Scholz is gonna get
selected at scrum-half.
Be a pal, Jack. Help me
work it so I play
fullback.

PATRICK (NARROWING EYES)
What did ya have in
mind?

INT. AUSTIN'S HOTEL ROOM - NIGHT

Coaches and captains discuss the final roster. Puffing a cigar, Austin brings up O'Neil's weeping surgical incision.

AUSTIN
What if O'Neil comes
out 'cause of his
stomach?

COLBY
He's all grit, coach. He won't.

Austin agrees. Peters reports that the doctor cleared Lefty to play. Austin moves to keep Lefty; Roe reluctantly agrees.

AUSTIN
Good. Now... scrum half. Sorry, Charlie. Lookin' like we gotta put Scholz at 9.

ROE (BELLOWING)
What?! I started four years at Stanford. And I helped YOU win in Antwerp.

Roe turns and points at Colby.

ROE
And YOU too!

AUSTIN
Pipe down, Roe!

COLBY
Charlie, it's not your fault the pack can't push.

ROE

Damn right! It's Mannelli and Dud's.

COLBY

Not really. We asked guys from other sports to join the team. It's nobody's fault they've not been scrumming long.

Austin grunts and nods. Roe sneers but says nothing.

COLBY

We need Rudy at scrum half. He's the only guy who can shag the wild balls. And the pushing problem isn't his fault either.

AUSTIN

I'd put you at fullback, Charlie, but Patrick's got just as much experience. And he's bigger. (beat) Could make you our extra man fringing round the scrum... *free fringer.*

COLBY

I think it would be better to put Norman at free

fringer. He may be a peach off the field, but I wouldn't choose to run a back row ploy around his side of the scrum.

LEWIS
I think you're right, Colby.

Austin grunts again and writes on his clipboard. Roe suppresses a wry smile.

INT. PIERRE'S OFFICE - DAY

THIS SCENE IS SPOKEN IN FRENCH WITH ENGLISH SUBTITLES.

Pierre paces in front of his office window, hand clenched behind his back. Seated nearby at a desk, Muhr looks on.

MUHR
You can't control the emotion of the common people, Pierre.

Pierre continues pacing, not looking at Muhr.

PIERRE (EMPHATIC)
They are showing disrespect rather than unity and mutual admiration.

MUHR

Yes, it's unpleasant at times, the human condition. What can we do?

PIERRE

The Jesuits taught me that every person is to be respected as a child of God. In proper rugby culture, everyone possesses a similar dignity and is treated accordingly.

Muhr waits, realizing that Pierre is utterly engrossed in his own thoughts and won't be reasoned with.

PIERRE

Take this down and release it to the press immediately. The very soul of the game is at stake.

Muhr takes a deep breath and picks up a pen.

MUHR

As you wish, Baron.

PIERRE

"The Olympic Committee asks the public to abstain from all demonstrations, and counts on the public's good will to aid in the success of the Games..."

Muhr dutifully writes.

EXT. VACANT LOT - DAY

Practice is in full-swing on the lot. Along with scrumming, the Americans practice line-outs, penalties, rucks, mauls, and kick-offs.

The scrum evolves. Norman does the put ins so Rudy can stay back in *shotgun*. Over with the backs, Peters critiques.

PETERS

You need to be able to field all kicks like that one, Jack.

Patrick grunts an acknowledgement, then walks over to Austin, squinting. He says he's been having trouble with light sensitivity and worries he'll struggle to field kicks at fullback during the gold game. Patrick says his antagonistic disposition might be better suited to the new free fringer position rather than fullback anyway. Austin nods pensively. Roe sees them talking and smiles. Later,

Colby is agitated that Norman has been benched and replaced by Patrick.

O'Neil retreats to the sideline to rub Sloan's Liniment on his infected surgical incision. Lewis notices.

LEWIS
Careful, gonna turn yourself blue.

O'NEIL
I'm not planning on using it after the final.

LEWIS
Got the sickness?

O'NEIL
You mean the infection?

LEWIS (KNOWINGLY)
I mean the rugby.

Pedestrians heckle the team as they practice. The team ignores them. Glarner, on the scene with Photographer 1, interviews passers-by at the curb in front of the lot.

A shop keeper adjacent to the lot watches the practice with a few of his workers and buddies. They mumble to each other and some loiterers, scheming.

The group from the shop carries scaffolding around from behind the building and begins assembling it so it encroaches on the practice area. They also carry a bucket, rags, and squeegee over, though the second floor is clearly abandoned and a simple ladder would have sufficed for window washing. The group heads back behind the building for more pieces.

Colby watches, then walks over to the first tier of braced scaffold bucks (see Apx. C pic). Glarner pushes past some prattling locals and asks Colby for a statement. Colby calmly agrees as he unhitches a cross-brace from the bucks.

GLARNER

How are you feeling about the match against France?

COLBY

I'm proud of our team. We're going to show up and give it everything we have. Too bad the French players can't show the same respect for the game. I hear your star, Jaureguy, has gone on vacation instead of competing.

Colby neatly leans the bucks against the masonry shop wall, then grabs a brace and casually launches it up onto the roof of a one-story addition without breaking eye contact with Glarner. Disturbed pigeons flutter loudly away.

As Glarner is scribbling notes, the group returns with more bucks and braces. Colby turns, eyes wide in challenge. A flashbulb goes off. They see the disassembled scaffolding, look at each other, and leave. Photographer 1 winds his camera. Glarner finishes writing and then extends his hand.

GLARNER

Thank you very much. It will be in tomorrow's paper.

INT. FRENCH VILLA - DAY

THIS SCENE IS SPOKEN IN FRENCH WITH ENGLISH SUBTITLES.

Adolphe Jaureguy eats breakfast in a gorgeous, sun-filled room in his French Villa on the Riviera. A beautiful, meticulously dressed and groomed woman strolls in from outside. SALOME is carrying a folded newspaper with her fingertips, like it's dirty and bothersome.

Without looking at Jaureguy or speaking to him, she drops it abruptly on the table in front of him and keeps walking.

Jaureguy rolls his eyes and says something under his breath. He glances at the paper and reads while he continues to eat. Suddenly, he drops his knife and grabs the paper, pulling it closer to his face. There's a picture of Colby by the vacant lot and a headline that includes Jaureguy's name. Jaureguy throws the paper down and smacks the table violently.

JAUREGUY
Merde! Salome!
SALOME!!

Salome replies nonchalantly from another room.

JAUREGUY
Get my suitcase! I've got
to go back to Paris.

Salome comes into the room, pouting and huffy.

SALOME
Paris? If you leave I
won't be here when you
return.

Jaureguy looks up, glaring, as he lights a cigarette. He gets up violently from the table and disappears into another room, making lots of loud banging and slamming noises. He reappears, holding a pink suitcase, and drops it abruptly in front of her like she dropped the paper. Without a word, he turns around and disappears again. She's speechless.

INT. SLATER FARM - KITCHEN - DAY

Louise and Marguerite step into the kitchen from outside, sweaty and dirty from farm work. Marguerite is carrying the mail. She tosses everything onto the counter except for a letter with Colby's name on the return address.

LOUISE
Don't smudge all over it!

Marguerite makes a show of wiping her hands thoroughly on her bandanna. Then she opens the letter and looks at it silently, her eyes running down the page.

LOUISE
Out loud!

MARGUERITE
"May 6th! Dear mother..." AND my wonderful, self-sacrificial sister.

Marguerite pauses, waiting for a laugh. Instead, Louise bites her lip and opens her eyes wide in anticipation.

MARGUERITE
"I have lost all ambition to write." Well, I'VE lost all ambition to feed your chickens.

LOUISE
Marguerite. Please.

Marguerite reads on, reaching the part in Colby's letter where he mentions his sore thumb.

MARGUERITE
Sore thumb? I've got scabs on all ten digits and peck marks on every freckle!

LOUISE
MARGO!

Marguerite continues, becoming more serious as she reads about the hopelessness of the American team playing against France. She pauses and swallows when Colby talks about giving the French a David and Goliath battle anyway. At the end of the letter, when Colby asks Louise to give his best to everyone, a tear runs down Louise's cheek and Marguerite's eyes have become glassy. The women stand in silence for a while, then make eye contact and laugh at their mutual tears and anxious expressions.

MARGUERITE
Don't worry, Ma. Colby is a force of nature when he's riled up. Albert says he wouldn't want to fight him, even with two friends. Colby'll be fine.

Marguerite hands Louise the letter.

MARGUERITE
Here. I'm going to go tend to some hungry chickens.

INT. BUS - DAY

One large Renault bus with solid rubber tires bumps roughly along a Parisian street, transporting the 23 American players, three coaches and one trainer to Colombes Stadium.

Austin rides in the front driver's compartment, sweating profusely. The nearby DRIVER mops his forehead. No one speaks amid the rumbling and squeaking of the bus.

Peters sits in the front right seat. The bus hits a particularly big pothole and Peters grabs the rail with his two-fingered left hand. He holds steady, but the driver's le coq gaulois (French rooster) charm suspended from the rear-view mirror swings wildly.

Once the bus stops rocking, Peters turns around, squinting to see through the reflected light. Behind him, the players are sleeping, staring down or staring out the windows. Their faces shine with sweat. Peters turns forward again and sighs, a faint smile growing on his face. (See Apx. B shot.)

The bus nears Colombes Stadium. O'Neil watches Hyland, a row ahead of him, frown up at the grand, imposing stadium already filling with spectators.

EXT. COLOMBES STADIUM - DAY [CONTINUOUS]

The players' solemn, anxious faces loom in the bus's windows.

TITLE OVER: May 18, 1924 - Rugby Final: USA vs. France

A massive, mostly French crowd has gathered. The atmosphere is electric. On the field, a French military band plays the Olympic Hymn. A huge French flag flies overhead.

To the right of the announcer box is a smaller box for the French local radio broadcaster. To the left, one for the ENGLISH BROADCASTER.

BROADCASTER
Wow! There's upwards of 21,000 people in the stands today despite the unusually sweltering heat.

SERIES OF SHOTS:

-Waiter discretely listens to radio at the hotel

-Doorman busts Waiter

-The Quins, including STOOP and CURRIE (on crutches), gather around a radio at Bedford Tavern imploring its ENGLISH BARTENDER to adjust the AM tuning to minimize static

-Cars pack the designated parking area for the stadium and overflow out onto the streets

-Hubbub as people try to move among the packed stands

-Gideon climbs the stands before asking if he can sit next to Lucia and Luella

-A GENDARMES CAPTAIN frowns at workers finishing the last section of crowd fence extensions

-AOA Member 1 is escorted to an area reserved for American dignitaries

Jaureguy makes his entrance. Fans respond with thunderous applause. From his VIP box, Pierre also waves proudly to the crowd. The French team begins to assemble into a line, hands behind their backs. Lasserre stands in front of the line.

BROADCASTER
The crowd is going wild for French star Adolphe Jaureguy, who wasn't expected to be here today. And it looks like the American team will be taking the field momentarily...

CUT TO:

INT. UNDERGROUND LOCKER ROOM - SAME

The U.S. Olympic rugby team waits in the locker room below the stadium. They're anxious and quiet in the muffled din. Lefty taps the strange object he holds. O'Neil absentmindedly rubs his abdomen. Several players, including Dud, lay flat on their backs on the cool concrete. A B-SIDE PLAYER spontaneously offers his scrum cap to cap-less Valentine.

AUSTIN
Time to line up, boys.

TUNNEL

Colby walks past each of his teammates lining the wall of the tunnel. His cleats clink against concrete, echoing. He recounts the disrespect and disparagement Americans have faced since leaving California. He points out the diversity of the players he passes, and how they will persevere as specialized parts working powerfully together as one body.

He pauses by Rudy, towering at 6'3" over the 5'6" lawyer. A loud *scrippp* echoes through the tunnel as Trainer, wearing a vertically striped jacket, pulls tape.

COLBY
I know more about
lettuce than lawyering.

But on the pitch Rudy
and I aren't so different.

Colby then reveals he's spent half his life trying to forget the death of his step-dad. His mom, Norman, Peters, Lucia, Rudy, the coaches and rugby brothers have inspired him to start healing and living again. It's difficult for him to face his traumas, but also a relief. Reaching the end of the line, Colby reverses direction.

A MUSTACHED FRENCH OFFICIAL's voice echoes from the field at the top of the tunnel staircase.

MUSTACHED OFFICIAL (IN FRENCH)
Time to go!

CUT TO:

EXT. COLOMBES STADIUM - SAME

The noise from the band blends with the noise of the crowd. Tension heightens as the French team stoically waits for the Americans to emerge.

BACK TO:

INT. UNDERGROUND LOCKER ROOM - SAME

COLBY (SWALLOWING)
I'm supposed to lead you
as captain. But whether
you knew it or not,
you've been leading me

out of my own darkness.
Thank God for you
guys... and for rugby.

Cheers emit from numerous players.

COLBY

Your determination has
gotten me, and all of us,
this far. Now it's time to
finish what we started.
(beat) Gentlemen, let's
show 'em the États Unis
is in town.

The players yell in agreement, jogging together through the tunnel and up the stairs to the cacophony of their cleats.

BACK TO:

EXT. COLOMBES STADIUM - DAY

A hush comes over the crowd as Mustached Official steps back from the tunnel stairway railing. Following Colby, the Americans jog up the steps and onto the field. (See Apx. B shot.) Both film crews push to get good position. Mustached Official takes an additional step back as Lefty emerges wearing a terrifying mask-like nose guard.

Colby and Lasserre meet the referee, Freethy, on the field for the coin toss. From the vantage point of the field,

Colby can see just how massive the crowd is. His face is impassive. The French win the coin toss.

LASSERRE (IN FRENCH)
We elect to receive.

Lasserre turns to Colby.

LASSERRE (IN BROKEN ENGLISH)
Tell your *rugby players*
do not blink.

Colby maintains his impassive expression. The captains shake hands and trot back to their teams.

Patrick kicks-off to the French to start the game. The Americans, tired of being dissed, make every hit count as the game gets underway. They refuse to give an inch in the early clashes. French players and fans are taken aback at the strength of the American tackles.

Portly Cameraman and an IOC CAMERAMAN jockey for position on the field, hip-checking while each struggles to hold his heavy equipment. They have to be agile and alert not to tangle their camera cords or get in the way of players.

The Americans have a few good runs but can't manage to score due to quick French defenders. Though outnumbered 30 to 1, the American fans are on their feet cheering.

The game settles into a series of punts for field position. Finally, Farish gets a break and makes an astonishing run, diving into the try-zone to the right of the posts to score. French center, JEAN VAYSSE, throws a cheap-shot haymaker in an attempt to make Farish muff his dot-down. (See Apx. B shot.) In the stands, the American crowd goes wild. Lucia and Gideon turn to each other in shock, then cheer at the tops of their lungs. Farish angrily points at Vaysse. The scoreboard displays 3-0.

O'Neil grabs Farish's jersey in celebration, coaxing a shy smile out of the rookie. Roe misses the conversion, causing the French to jeer, but the cheering Americans don't care.

On the sideline, Austin mutters to Lewis that the French are favored 20 to 1. He glances at the scoreboard, pleased. Peters calls Devereaux towards the sideline for some tips, pointing-out that French fly-half HENRI GALAU has been *cheating-forward* on defense. Peters suggests a dummy pass to keep Galau *honest*. Patrick kicks off. The French players are shocked and angry at the American score. In the stands, agitated French fans drown out the American cheers with hissing and booing.

In his box, Pierre looks disturbed, gazing out over the loud and disorderly fans.

The 3-4 scrum is starting to work. In response, French players resort to dirty play, throwing elbows and knees at the American players. The French target Colby, trying to provoke retaliation, but he and the other Americans are able to show restraint. Devereaux fakes Galau out of his jock.

Despite being small and injured, O'Neil shows no fear in facing larger French players. Rudy is also fearless, tackling and being tackled by much larger men.

Finally, Jaureguy is fed a ball and makes a break.

BROADCASTER
Jaureguy is flying! He's in the open with the ball, putting on speed and leaving Americans behind. It looks like this might be the French answer to Farish's try.

A white uniform angles forward, head down and accelerating. With a sickening crunch, the man in the mask slams into Jaureguy and knocks him off his feet. Jaureguy remains on the ground, writhing. Shocked, the crowd falls silent.

Rudy pulls Lefty to the side as several of Jaureguy's teammates rush to him. Lefty adjusts his nose guard.

Angry French players flock to the referee to protest the hit. Freethy shakes his head and motions them back. Lasserre herds his teammates away, except Lubin as interpreter. Only then, and as Lasserre and Lubin approach Freethy respectfully, does the referee discuss the legality of Lefty’s hit.

BROADCASTER
It appears referee
Freethy won't call a
penalty on that hit. The
French players aren't
happy at all with that.

Slowly, with help, Jaureguy gets back up. The crowd cheers. As the match resumes, French play gets dirtier.

Soon, the French star gets another break. 25 yards from the try-zone, he looks like he's home-free when Valentine comes barreling seemingly out of nowhere. The 210 pound linebacker crashes into Jaureguy so hard it knocks him out cold. In the stands, Lucia's cheer dies in her throat. Jaureguy's upper lip is split and bleeding as he lies unconscious.

Medics rush to Jaureguy, who remains unconscious. The stands are eerily hushed. The French fans are shocked and horrified, and the Americans sense danger. Blood soaks into Jaureguy's jersey as he's carried off the field, allowing play to resume. With a roar, fighting commences in the stands and several French fans attempt to climb over the extended crowd fence. Gendarmes respond, pulling the climbers down and away from the pitch.

BROADCASTER
Referee Freethy's
whistle signals the end of
the first half of play. The

Americans, underdogs in this contest, have surprised everyone by leading France 3-0.

Though he's been confined to the sidelines, Turk is still encouraging to his teammates as they break for halftime.

TURK

Alright, boys, you can do this! They're worried so we gotta give them a big second half! A real big half!

American players lie flat on the grass, catching their breath and nursing their wounds. Assistant coaches and reserves pass water around and help wrap ankles, wrists, and knees. Trainer rubs salve into Dixon's shoulder (See Apx. B shot.)

Roe is distracted by the continuing din from the crowd. He chastises Valentine.

ROE

Why'd you have to hit him that hard, Valentine? These people are gonna dismember us!

Austin gets everyone's attention.

AUSTIN

Listen up! I've never seen a squad so top to bottom on the same hymn sheet. It's a slim lead. But it shows your focus. Your discipline. But French honor's on the line. You gotta play even harder and faster.

Austin's voice raises.

AUSTIN

And you gotta play clean no matter what. They're cracking. Keep it up and they'll collapse.

The whistle blows, signaling the end of halftime. Despite the risk to their own safety, American fans cheer wildly as their team takes the field again. The team is touched and heartened by the support.

BROADCASTER

The Americans come into the second half with a razor-thin 3-point lead. France kicks off.

During the first ten minutes of the second half, the Americans keep the ball almost exclusively in French territory. But as the game progresses, smooth and efficient French teamwork starts to balance out play again. Lasserre solidly tackles Devereaux, shutting down another dummy. French confidence returns, but their self-control wavers.

During a ruck, a DIRTY FRENCH PLAYER notices a spot of blood seeping through O'Neil's jersey and rakes his stomach. O'Neil is left on the grass in a ball. Dupont bobbles the ball.

FREETHY (WHISTLING)
That's a knock. Scrum white. I suggest calling it a day, 2.

An American fan named PAT HIGGINS from Los Angeles pushes through the stands to the crowd fence. He's smashed up against it as he yells encouragement to the team.

PAT
Keep going, boys! You've got 'em beat!

O'Neil is red in the face and sick with pain. He manages to roll over onto his knees and spot Pat. His face brightens. Panting through clenched teeth and unable to speak, O'Neil hauls himself to his feet and lifts his arms out, signaling to his props that he's ready to continue scrumming.

Minutes later, Rudy gains possession and perfectly times a pass to Colby running in support. Colby plants a devastating stiff-arm before racing away, using his power and long legs to plow straight through a few French players to score. But Freethy disallows the try, calling Rudy for a knock-on.

Rudy helps Colby to his feet and gives him a handshake, grinning widely.

RUDY

That was gorgeous!

Later, during a line-out, O'Neil throws the ball to Dud who charges forward, creating a platform for a maul. Patrick rolls-out of the maul 30 yards from the try zone. He makes it past five French players to score a try, then plants the ball between the posts. Roe converts. The scoreboard shows 8-0.

In spite of threats and warnings to keep quiet from French fans, a few young American fans, including Gideon, lead a brave cheering section. They perform The Charleston. A FRENCH ARISTOCRAT whips his gold-tipped cane with a whoosh, cutting a gash over Gideon's ear. Lucia witnesses this and sees Gideon drop to the ground. She pushes through to him.

Dixon crosses the try-line but forgets to touch the ball down. He's tackled by three French players and fails to score. Farish gets another try on an impressive 40-yard run. In the conversion attempt, the ball hits the crossbar. The scoreboard reads 11-0.

A high punt lands near the USA try line and neither Dixon nor Roe catch it cleanly. Roe is reduced to spectator after letting the ball bounce. Galau falls on it to claim a try. BEHOTEGUY misses the conversion drop-kick and the scoreboard shows 11-3.

Lubin, fired up and irrational, blatantly punches Colby. He's sent off the field immediately. Colby appeals to Freethy, not wanting the French team to play with more of a handicap than they've already got with Jaureguy gone. Freethy agrees to reinstate Lubin. However, Lubin is seething and refuses to return. Finally, Colby puts his arm on Lubin's back and kindly encourages him off the bench, settling the matter.

Leaping high, Colby steals a line-out that should have been won by the French. This unleashes Cleaveland to begin a passing rush that sweeps the Americans all the way down the field. Lefty scores, grinning roguishly behind his nose guard. Roe is stuck with a nearly impossible angle to convert, and consequently misses. The scoreboard reads 14-3.

Finally, O'Neil hooks the ball out clean. Rudy controls it and, with astonishing agility, runs around the scrum and under Lasserre's reaching arm. (See Apx. B shot.)

VALENTINE (WITH GUSTO)
Go G-man!

Colby, looking on, finally smiles.

In the ensuing passing rush, Caesar Mannelli scores the last try of the game. Roe's drop-kick hits the crossbar again. A whistle blow ends the game.

BROADCASTER
And that's it, ladies and gents! America wins the gold, defeating heavily favored France 17 to 3!

The American team looks up at the scoreboard, dumbfounded.

SERIES OF SHOTS:

-Back in Hotel Exelmans, Doorman and Waiter secretly hug in celebration

-The Harlequins cheer loudly and toast across the Channel

-The American flag rises up above the French and Romanian flags for the medal ceremony

Chaos breaks out as the French fans attack more American fans. Gendarmes attempt to intercede. Turk gets up and heads for the line of French players.

CAESAR
Hey, where are you going?

TURK
It's a tradition. You give your jersey to the other

team. They give you one
in return. Be right back...

Turk takes both hands and pulls up his white jersey over his head to trade with Dupont. At that moment, a HATEFUL FRENCH FAN behind Dupont breaks through the line of gendarmes and kicks Turk in the groin. His head still covered with the jersey, Turk crumples onto the ground in agony.

Valentine spots Lucia following FRENCH MEDICS carrying Gideon on a stretcher. Gideon's head has been bandaged, though blood still shows on his face and in his hair. Valentine grabs Dud and the two of them relieve MEDIC 1 and MEDIC 2 of the stretcher, freeing them up to care for more injuries. The Americans head for the safety of the tunnel.

The French band begins playing La Marseillaise, but it's hard to hear over the riot noise. Gendarmes hold back aggressive French fans while the French team is awarded their silver medals. As the band begins playing the Star-Spangled Banner to award the Americans their gold medals, the crowd roars and the attacks surge. O'Neil, standing alone, fearlessly salutes the American flag. Fans are hurling anything they can get their hands on. The line of gendarmes keeping rioters off the field starts to collapse. Pierre shakes his head in disbelief, tears welling in his eyes.

PIERRE (IN FRENCH)
I have created a monster.

Seeing a crisis quickly evolving, Dupont hesitates for a moment, then rushes to help the gendarmes holding back rioters. Other French players see him and gradually follow suit. Gendarmes Captain calls off the gold medal ceremony and gathers a group of his men to escort the Americans down to their locker room, joined by some French players.

Because of his abdominal wound, O'Neil has to be propped up as the group moves toward the locker room. Farish looks lost and stunned by the chaos around him. He's swept along into the tunnel by his teammates and the gendarmes.

INT. UNDERGROUND LOCKER ROOM - DAY

The American team takes refuge. Both the tunnel and locker room entrances are blocked by gendarmes. Howling and angry noises filter in from outside.

COLBY
Your idea worked.
Congratulations.

RUDY
Well, you got one hell of
a team.

COLBY
WE got one hell of a
team.

American dignitaries and officials squeeze through the gendarmes' barricade into the tunnel. AOA Member 1 shakes hands with Austin, congratulating him. Austin pulls AOA Member 1 close so that he can be heard over the ruckus.

AUSTIN (WINKING)
Boys took
their *beatings*... like
gentlemen.

Austin claps him on the shoulder roughly and moves on. Glarner also pushes his way down into the American locker room to witness the celebration. He begins to write, "...our men were too frail...could not hold up to the admirable athletes before them."

On a bench in the locker room, Gideon stirs. Lucia tends to his bandages with Valentine hovering anxiously behind her. Gideon begins to groggily peer at Valentine above him.

GIDEON
Heavens, Lucia. I take a
quick nap and you leave
me for a goon?

Lucia smiles wryly.

LUCIA
Well, he’s not just any
goon.

Valentine blushes deeply but looks pleased.

POP! Colby's head whips around at the loud sound of a champagne bottle being opened. He takes a deep breath and stays composed.

Austin pours celebratory glasses and Lewis and Peters pass them out. There's a commotion in the tunnel.

CAESAR
They want you, Colby.

Unsure, Colby makes his way over to the locker room door. There stands Lasserre and the one-eyed Lubin. Colby and Lasserre confront one another. After a tense pause, Lubin puts out a conciliatory hand.

LUBIN
Apologies for our behavior. We congratulate you.

Lasserre addresses Colby, and Lubin interprets.

LUBIN (FOR LASSERRE)
We fought as comrades in the Great War. We should not part with bad feelings. And we are rugby men, men of honor. Your team played very well. You beat us fairly.

Colby nods and shakes hands with both Frenchmen. Retreating to the locker room, his eyes meet Peters'. They exchange knowing looks. They're living again.

INT. LIDO DES CHAMPS ELYSEES - NIGHT

TITLE OVER: Lido des Champs Elysees - Five days later

From a swimming pool (see Apx. C pic) in the middle of the restaurant, Caesar responds a little too enthusiastically to a champagne toast. Twenty feet away a thin, slightly hunched man yells from the team table.

O'NEIL

Criminy, Mannelli, you splashed a lady!

CUT TO VIDEO EPILOGUE (V.E.) 1 - O'Neil is seen climbing one of his oil derricks to help an employee. (See Apx. C pic.) He sputters and chuckles when some oil splashes on his face.

BACK TO RESTAURANT - Members of the French rugby team share drinks and revelry with Team USA, including Lasserre, Dupont, and even Adolphe Jaureguy. Seated next to Hyland, Jaureguy smiles and celebrates enthusiastically despite his stitched and swollen lip.

CUT TO V.E. 2 - Jaureguy and Hyland ride towards The Riviera in a Chendard & Walcker (see Apx. C) convertible, both wearing Stade Français rugby club gear.

BACK TO RESTAURANT - Gathering drinks from the bar for his teammates, Turk respectfully declines a PRETTY FRENCH WOMAN's offer to dance. When he attempts to pay, the FRENCH BARTENDER raises his hands and shakes his head.

CUT TO V.E. 3 - Turk puffs with anxiety, holding his hat on as he rounds the last corner into the San Francisco park overlooking the bay. He stops, breathless, as he spots a distant figure waiting for him on the bench.

TITLE OVER: Elaine and Turk enjoyed a 69-year marriage.

CUT TO V.E. 4 - Turk and Elaine are having wedding photos taken. A WEDDING PHOTOGRAPHER shoots the couple, then asks Turk to step away to take a solo shot of Elaine. Turk looks taken aback for a moment. He quickly recovers and steps away.

TURK

Of course, of course. But please hurry so I can return to her side.

Wedding Photographer snaps the photo of Elaine. (Morph to actual wedding photo from Apx. C.)

TITLE OVER: Turk entered the San Francisco Police Academy, worked his way up and eventually became commissioner.

BACK TO RESTAURANT - Seated beside each other at the team table, Peters catches-up with his old opponent, Muhr. Muhr has an idea. He swallows quickly, slams his drink down, and puts up a finger. He starts to loosen his rugby tie as Peters puts his good hand out in respectful protest. Muhr gets the tie over his head and overrides the protest by stuffing it down Peters shirt, patting it with a warm smile.

CUT TO V.E. 5 - An older Muhr looks up as he hears a knock at his doorway, the same doorway where Peters revealed himself two decades earlier. Muhr says to come in and the secretary lets two SS OFFICERS into Muhr's office.

TITLE OVER: During WWII, Allan Muhr of Philadelphia was taken to a German concentration camp where he perished.

TITLE OVER: France posthumously awarded Muhr the Legion d'Honneur. (Insert photo of Muhr from Apx. C.)

CUT TO V.E. 6 - Peters is back at the Dockyard now working on the inside of the door. He checks his watch before chucking his tools into his toolbox. CUT TO a stadium shot with Peters seated next to Stoop. As Peters unbuttons his coat we see that he's wearing Muhr's tie. (Insert 1906 photo of French and English players including Muhr and Peters from Apx. C.)

BACK TO RESTAURANT - Two LOITERING FRENCHMEN, one TALL and the other SHORT, are smoking outside the Lido. Short holds a newspaper.

Valentine walks by and Short nudges Tall, whispering excitedly in French. Short points to Valentine's face at the top of a newspaper article that features a photo of the American rugby team. Glarner's name is visible.

CUT TO V.E. 7 - Valentine and Lucia have a beautiful wedding.

TITLE OVER: Lucia and Valentine married in 1928.

TITLE OVER: Valentine became president of University of Rochester at age 34. There, he conferred honorary doctorate degrees to both George Washington Carver and Sir Winston Churchill. (Insert photos of Valentine, Lucia and Valentine and Carver, from Apx. C.)

BACK TO RESTAURANT - Colby smiles as Rudy tells the 3-4 story in animated fashion, using coins on the table.

CUT TO V.E. 8 - Rudy returns to his law practice, marries MILDRED, and has four sons. An elderly man throws a pass during an old boys game. (Freeze frame morph to photo of Rudy at 83 years old from Apx. C.)

CUT TO V.E. 9 - Colby revisits Belgium to honor his fallen friends. (Insert photo of Colby in WWI uniform from Apx. C.) Colby returns home to Woodland and his farming life.

CUT TO V.E. 10 - Years later (c. 1939) there's a knock at the Slater Farm door.

COLBY
I've got it, Virginia!

As the door opens three boys push-in. They are led by the oldest, ten-year-old RUD SCHOLZ. The boys are followed by their mother carrying a baby. Rud trots over to six-year-old MARYLIN SLATER asking if he can play with her doll. Marylin pauses before handing over the figure wearing a scrum cap and a jersey bearing an American flag emblem.

COLBY (SMILING)
Welcome, Mildred.
Who's this?

MILDRED
This is David.

Colby admires DAVID SCHOLZ and shakes hands with Rudy, congratulating him on the new son. David promptly spits up on himself. Colby shoots into the kitchen to grab a towel, stumbling upon Norman sticking his head into the ice box. Colby suppresses a smile.

COLBY
I don't remember inviting
you to come over and eat
all my food.

NORMAN
Tell it to Sweeney.

Colby returns to the living room where the Scholz family has settled. He grins at Rudy as he hands Mildred the towel.

COLBY
Only eleven more and you've got a team, G-Man. Congratulations.

RUD
What's G-Man mean, Daddy?

RUDY
It means this lug--I mean Mr. Slater--loves me.

THE END

[Incorperate additional epilogues:]

LEFTY ROGERS' nose healed. He earned a medical degree from Stanford and became a surgeon. In 1969 Lefty started The Second Opinion, a charity to help ensure accurate diagnoses for cancer patients. (Insert Apx. C picture.)

CAESAR MANNELLI leveraged his degree from Santa Clara University and became an engineer for the City of San Francisco. He died in a construction accident, leaving behind his wife, Mary. Caesar was 39. (Insert Apx. C picture)

LUELLA MELIUS Repeated her role as Gilda in Chicago during the 1925-26 season. She went on to enjoy a radio broadcasting career for BBC, and also in America. (Insert Apx. C pictures: At piano; with Team USA; with Team France in sweaters.)

Stanford All-American football player DUD DEGROOT pursued a career in coaching. He held head positions at West Virginia University, University of New Mexico, and with the Washington Redskins, among others. (Insert Apx. C picture)

ALBERT FREETHY was a first-class cricketeer from Wales. After retiring from cricket, Freethy became one of rugby's greatest and most respected referees of the era, watching over 18 internationals. (Insert Apx. C picture.) Freethy on Team USA:

"With several more weeks of training, they could beat any team in Europe, not barring the best of the British Isles."

MARGUERITE MESSENGER was among the bright young agricultural pioneers who developed the Imperial Valley. Combining "brains, enthusiasm and hard work," the Messengers found success during the Valley's tumultuous times after the flooding of the diverted Colorado River and before the digging of All-American Canal. (Insert Apx. C picture.)

Weeks after the rugby finals, ERIC LIDDELL refused to run the 100-meter dash because the heats were held on a Sunday. He would not compromise his religious beliefs surrounding the Sabbath. Liddell then won bronze in the 200-meter dash as Jackson Scholz took the gold. Finally, Liddell won gold in the 400. After the Olympics, he returned to China as a missionary. During WWII he refused to evacuate and died in a Japanese prison camp. (Insert Apx. C picture)

ADRIAN STOOP played rugby for the Harlequins until he was 56. Their stadium, built in 1963, is named Twickenham Stoop Stadium in his honor. (Insert Apx. C picture)

LINN FARISH joined the OSS, the precursor to the CIA. During WWII he was assigned missions in the Balkans. Despite his high intelligence, Farish was duped into sharing incorrect intel with the Pentagon and White House. Consequently, American weapons and supplies were used by the Partisans to commit massacres. Upon learning the truth, Farish had a break-down. His pleas to talk to FDR again were rejected. Unable to cope with these murders, involving innocent women and children, Farish continuously volunteered to fly suicide missions until his small plane did not return. He was posthumously awarded the Distinguished Service Cross, and later accused of being a Soviet spy. (Insert Apx. C picture)

PIERRE DE COUBERTIN never recovered emotionally from his own personal traumas, or financially from personally funding so many Olympics between 1896 and 1924. After the rugby riot, Pierre left the IOC and France. Following the events in Paris, Pierre's successors banned rugby from the Olympics for 92 years.

Late in life Pierre wrote from Switzerland about his work, describing it as an *unfinished symphony*.

"Every human being... belongs to the great orchestra of mankind. Most of us, it must be admitted, play a very minor role. Not everyone is able to fit in; some never succeed in finding their place. Very few are favored by fate to the extent of being allowed to compose pieces themselves. Rarer still are those who are privileged to hear them performed during their lifetime."

Cut-off financially by his wife, Pierre died bitter and poor in Geneva in 1937. As requested in his will, his heart was removed and placed in a marble column in Olympia, Greece, the birthplace of the Olympics. (Insert Apx. C picture)

[Incorperate PTSD information:]

Since the onset of the 21st century, veteran suicides have increased 31 percent, and suicides among U.S. civilian adults have increased 24 percent (U.S. Department of Veteran Affairs, 2016). Post-Traumatic Stress Disorder (PTSD) has often been associated with the 21st century U.S. suicide epidemic and other sufferings of veterans, survivors of sexual assault, and victims of other extreme trauma.

Visit https://www.ptsd.va.gov if you or someone you know might be suffering from PTSD.

[Incorperate Fall 2017 / Spring 2018 HG Internal Reviewers:]

Luke Agness, P.J. Harris, Brian Homet, Allie Norris, Morgan Pflug, Peter Pflug, Jeff Platenberg, Scott Stephens, B.D. Valle, Jeff Wargo, Kathy Young and Jeffrey Dillenbeck (captain)

[Incorperate *Keep Going* excerpt:]

"You did not ask to be born, but you are here. You have weaknesses as well as strengths. You have both because in life there is two of everything. Within you is the will to win, as well as the willingness to lose. Within you is the heart to feel compassion as well as the smallness to be arrogant. Within you is the way to face life as well as the fear to turn away from it...

Being strong means taking one more step toward the top of the hill, no matter how weary you may be. It means letting the tears flow through the grief. It means to keep looking for the answer, though the darkness of despair is all around you. Being strong means to cling to hope for one more heartbeat, one more sunrise. Each step, no matter how difficult, is one more step closer to the top of the hill. To keep hope alive for one more heartbeat at a time leads to the light of the next sunrise, and the promise of a new day. The weakest step toward the top of the hill, toward sunrise, toward hope, is stronger than the fiercest storm. Keep going."

-A Lakota Sioux grandfather to his grandson from *Keep Going: The Art of Perseverance*, by and with permission from Joseph M. Marshall III

Printed in Great Britain
by Amazon

51192443R00106